Fundamental Analysis

The Core Principles of Fundamental Analysis

(Using Fundamental Analysis & Fundamental Trading Techniques)

Esteban Schuler

D1737637

Published By **Zoe Lawson**

Esteban Schuler

Fundamental Analysis: The Core Principles of Fundamental Analysis (Using Fundamental Analysis & Fundamental Trading Techniques)

ISBN   978-1-77485-872-1

No part of this guidebook shall be reproduced in any form without permission in writing from the publisher except in the case of brief quotations embodied in critical articles or reviews.

Legal & Disclaimer

The information contained in this ebook is not designed to replace or take the place of any form of medicine or professional medical advice. The information in this ebook has been provided for educational & entertainment purposes only.

The information contained in this book has been compiled from sources deemed reliable, and it is accurate to the best of the Author's knowledge; however, the Author cannot guarantee its accuracy and validity and cannot be held liable for any errors or omissions. Changes are periodically made to this book. You must consult your doctor or get professional medical advice before using any of the suggested remedies, techniques, or information in this book.

TABLE OF CONTENTS

Introduction

Technical analysis is now an increasingly popular method to handle exchanges in part due to the development of charts as well as trading platform. For new traders knowing the basics of technical analysis and how it could aid in identifying patterns that are on the horizon--can be challenging and overwhelming.

Analysis of the technical aspects "analyzes" price fluctuations in a market. traders use notable charts and indicator patterns to anticipate future patterns based on their watch. It's a visual representation of the different times performance of a market. It allows traders to make use of this data as indicators of price activity as well as examples to guide and help future patterns to be taught prior to trading.

This basic technical analysis guide will help you understand the fundamentals of this

1

exchange technique and how it can be utilized to trade within the financial business sector.

The process of technical analysis involves the comprehension of the examples drawn from charts. The traders use important information based on the price and volume. They use this information to differentiate exchange openings based on the basic information in the search of. Diverse indicators are utilized on charts to determine when to segment and leave focus areas for traders to enhance the potential of a trade at high risk/reward ratios.

The underneath chart is an illustration of a chart with the utilization of the MACD (Moving Average Convergence/Divergence) and RSI (Relative Strength Index) indicators.

Although those who invest in technical analysis agree as true that the financial market is one of the main market participants Technical analysis traders are able to retain the same patterns from their previous studies to help anticipate future price fluctuations. While these exchange styles may be different, understanding the distinctions between technical and principal analysis, as well as how to connect them, can be extremely beneficial.

Chapter 1: What's The Fundamental

Analysis?

Every investor employs different strategies to attempt to predict the movement in the markets, and earn profit. One of the most popular techniques utilized by traders is known as Fundamental Analysis. No matter the amount of experience owned by the investor Fundamental Analysis explains, by using facts, what's happening in a particular financial market, in an attempt to predict what will occur to the trend in the following periods.

Many people have tried many occasions to venture into trade but lacking a actual market analysis or strategies for managing money the experience ended by failing. In reality, studying the information offered by research institutes and organizations is an ineffective strategy because the data is difficult to comprehend. A novice trader won't be able to make use of the information provided by these bodies, deciding on the right ones and putting them into an orderly manner.

What distinguishes Fundamental Analysis apart from any other method of market analysis is the capacity to determine a strategy not on the past or historical data instead, but on what's happening right now at the time you make your decision to invest.

So the Fundamental Analysis deals with observing and scrutinizing the current business trends to determine its potential to grow in the future and ways it can expand. So traders have an accurate view of the current market trends. However, it could be detrimental to base one's strategies solely in Fundamental Analysis. It is crucial for traders to combine the information and data derived from different analytical techniques in a manner that increases the probability of achieving success when it comes to the trading process.

But, it is also widely known that traders choose to completely ignore this type of analysis, instead focusing on different strategies. The first trader to enter the Forex market, or any other financial market employing fundamental analysis Fundamental Analysis can start off with other investors, but be able to compete with other traders and remain active in the market over the end.

This is why Fundamental Analysis does not focus on the obvious factors that make up trends, such as the cost of a particular financial instrument, or the potential profits earned from an investment, but can be based upon the research of the business as well as the value it can bring over time when properly optimized. This gives a broader perspective of the market that allows us to get rid of certain elements, which are sometimes crucial, which otherwise might be overlooked.

Fundamental Analysis Fundamental Analysis is generally oriented towards the future since it is not possible to determine what the direction of the trend could be in the near term as the business is a highly variable metric and is susceptible to seasonal changes in part because of the methods employed by businesses.

The Fundamental Analysis deals with analyzing and analyzing the state of health of an organization or investment asset. It is essential that the Fundamental Analysis must be applied consistently to be able to determine whether the health of the company is in good shape or whether the market is increasing or declining, and what are the implications of various economic factors on it. The trader needs to be aware of all factors that determine the economics and assets of the business, but also the performance of latter and can be assessed using a set of indices on the items which comprise those financial reports.

The Fundamental Analysis aims, according to the asset or company being that is being studied, to establish a number of goals that can aid the trader in making the right investment choices:

- - First the assessment of the business so that you can ensure higher probability of profit from the execution of long-term trading

Second, an evaluation of the macroeconomic trend that includes a detailed study of the factors pertaining to local production that could affect an asset's performance firm or asset

Thirdly, an analysis of the managerial and strategic decisions of every company that are capable of influencing the asset and also of the actions made by leaders of the political class and the impact of these decisions on the market

Then it is the thorough evaluation of the relation between risk and yield, by analyzing all the factors that may affect this relationship, and the analysis of the future events that may affect the relationship.

1.1 The main distinctions in Fundamental Analysis and Technical Analysis

Fundamental Analysis, or the Fundamental Analysis, for the features and the objects that are that are considered, is the exact opposite that is Technical Analysis. This is utilized by traders to analyze the past price trends of a specific financial instrument to determine if there is a correlation to the behaviour of the trend and, from this and the premise of what its future direction will be. This is why Technical Analysis Technical Analysis does not turn its attention to the financial and business statements, but instead concentrates its attention on prices and charts that illustrate how the price fluctuates of the same.

The whole Technical Analysis is based on the notion that all humans particularly those involved in the financial market, carry out their actions in a repetitive manner. This is due specifically to the notion that human behavior is driven by instinct. If the trend is positive an uncontrollable feeling of happiness prompts people to open up more positions. In contrast depression resulting from the inability of predicting the changes in the trend prompts traders to shut down positions. These two emotions, both completely unreal, are carried out in a monotonous fashion and push the trend either up or downwards. The Technical Analysis attempts to determine the state of mind of traders isin order to be able to predict the development that the market is experiencing.

The entire issue is not addressed in Fundamental Analysis. Fundamental Analysis, which focuses exclusively on data that has been published and made public by the statistical authorities , and those financial reports of various financial firms. The information is considered to be incomplete and needs to be analysed with the help of financial math.

Another distinction between the two kinds of analysis is defined by the time at which the decision to enter or exit of a market is made. Actually, the technical analyst waits for the moment of opening or closing of a position till the value has reached the value of a specific amount. This means that the trader needs to continuously and almost constantly observe the trends of the market as well as the change in the price. Another option is to depend on Trading System, that is automated systems that operate entirely independently in the financial market, on the base of the plan of action set by an investor. Fundamental Analysis Fundamental Analysis refers to two factors that are present in the market that are its actual worth as well as it's market value. When the value actually exceeds the market value the fundamental analyst is likely to open a new position in the market. The reverse is true the position has to be closed if the market value is greater than what is actually worth.

In depth, examining the two distinct strategies for the market, one could say that the analyst who is fundamental puts their efforts on the first phase of trading, which is the gathering of data and analyzing details, while a more extensive effort is required of analysts who specialize in technical analysis.

Moment of observation of the trend that is , during the period just prior to entering or leaving the market. In this case however, stress can quickly lead a trader into mistaken thinking that the market is too agitated, and choosing the perfect moment to make a choice could be extremely difficult.

However, in general it is not possible to establish a priori what is the best method of analysis between these two types, since each is tied to external influences and the risk tolerance of the investor. A skilled trader is aware of importance of both Technical and Fundamental Analyses are crucial for success in trading. Because of this the most effective option is to employ both depending on the circumstances or mix the two to improve your odds of earning profits.

Naturally regardless of the type of analysis that one chooses to use it is crucial to back each one by a proper strategy of managing risk and capital. In addition, the trader must always consider the fluctuation in markets and then on the basis all the elements decide on his preferred the investment.

The Technical Analysis and the Fundamental Analysis could be viewed as two different types of market analysis, but that's not the reason why traders shouldn't use both of them together. Actually, executing both kinds of analysis could provide advantages, since investors can gain an accurate picture of the market in the short - and medium-term as well as in the long time.

One of the most popular strategies employed by traders on both Forex as well as other markets for financial trading is to put an amount of money to the market and utilize it according to the guidelines laid out within the Technical Analysis, while the remaining portion should be invested according to the principles outlined within the Fundamental Analysis. It's a method of trying to make money in the short-termby using what is known as the Technical Analysis, and in the long run, by following what is known as the Fundamental Analysis.

1.2 What is the fundamental analysis for?

Fundamental Analysis is also used for other fields besides trading. For instance, many managers utilize the ideas that are a part of to this methodology to come up with forecasts that are likely but not sure about certain economic processes that are connected to their business. Through broadening the perspective of the world economy you can employ Fundamental Analysis for everyday choices and sometimes, even the smallest of choices that are a reflection of the daily lives of individuals. So the outlook for the coming years may be more stable and certain to be more luminous.

Fundamental analysis is also employed by workers. A worker in a company can study financial statements as well as all financial information that needs to be released in a compulsory manner to predict what the next steps of the business where he or she works , and consequently their future.

In general, entrepreneurs and professionals are also able to benefit from anticipating any crisis that might arise in the field. The ability to access and comprehend certain data can enable these individuals to look for ways to differentiate their business and in a manner to attract as many customers as is possible, and to deal with potential crisis in the most effective method.

Fundamental Analysis is also a method to determine the benefits that will come in the future associated with purchasing a durable product. No matter whether it's a corporation or a private company buying such a product is required to be properly weighted. However, an analysis like this could also be conducted by a selling business that analyzes the economic and financial possibilities of prospective customers. Additionally, many legal and physical subjects study the health status of financial institutions to figure out which one is the best where customers can deposit their money.

To realize the full potential of all this to realize all this, to realize all this, the Fundamental Analysis must be structured according to certain passages that, when done correctly can guarantee their complete efficacy.

One of the initial actions that any trader or anyone else has to undertake is the collection of data that will be subjected to analysis, related to a specific asset, to a business or financial institution. With the advent on the web, modern-day subjects can access the information needed for completing a study that is similar to this particularly by looking up the websites of different government agencies, both international and national institutions.

Another step is found in the surveys that are conducted by individuals who are interested directly in the areas of their activity. If the trader chooses to research the company in a manner that allows him to determine the likelihood of entering the market, he should visit the legal and financial offices of the various businesses which make up the business. They will determine what the actual flow of clients is, or the availability of goods to sell, or the ways of corporate structure used by the individual businesses.

When the visual and statistical information is gathered then the analyst who is in charge of them must divide them according to the nature of financial. In general, the data are divided into two categories that are the macroeconomic and the microeconomic. However, every person can choose to create an additional subdivision based on their specific needs. In order to accomplish this task you must use electronic worksheets.

But, the primary analyst must carry on the process of collecting data. It is essential to research all of the companies competing on their assets to determine the extent to which their health is, and most of all, their behavior. There are certain market periods that make firms appear to be aggressive and opening some financial positions in these times could be counterproductive. The data gathered should be used to establish comparisons, which are known to experts as benchmark.

In actuality the process of collecting data could be considered to be indefinite for those who choose to use Fundamental Analysis. In reality, once the historical and current data of businesses, competitors, and financial institutions are obtained, it will be an update and requires lesser effort than carrying through in the beginning stage of the research.

Certain fundamental analysts, particularly those who aren't experienced and do not know how to navigate or underestimate the actions. In the real world, without an accurate statistical foundation and an accurate view of the market's situation and the overall the health of competitors It is not possible to determine the value of the asset in relation to its value on the market, or to determine if one is in an era of under or overestimation of it.

This kind of approach will allow the fundamental analyst benefit more than any other area. But, this advantage has to be maintained throughout time through proper capital management, efficient risk management, and continuous update of data.

1.3 - - Data collection and analysis

As stated earlier the internet and numerous websites are the primary source of the patrimonial, statistical and economic information needed to make a valid Fundamental Analysis. It is therefore recommended to record each website in an economic calendar in which every date of the publication of data needed for analysis are listed.

In particular, the primary analyst should search for all financial policy announcements that relate to information or data, that are regularly released by the central banks. In addition, the quarterly information related to the trend of GDP which is what is known as the Gross Domestic Product of every country that indicate the health of the population and economic development, are crucial.

Additionally, depending on the kind that Fundamental Analysis carried out, it is required to gather data related to the the manufacturing sector alone and, therefore also, all production that doesn't originate from this industry specifically, the ones involves industries and the service or service sector. However, it is not just. It is essential not to undervalue the information related to the rate of the rate of inflation in a particular State which is an aspect that influences the trend in prices of the diverse assets, as well as those that pertain to the welfare and employment of a nation. The fundamental analyst should gather the information that allows to get the indices that reflect of the trust among consumers and companies, as well as the information that is reported on the balance sheets of companies , or other patrimonial and economic data which are released by institutions or the businesses regularly for example, data related to forecasts of the future trends in markets that are published through the European Commission.

It is also important to locate facts and figures that have not been scrutinized and reported by the media, because the asset or business situation might have changed, even if unintentionally. In other instances, the difficulty of finding data is due to the language differences and especially when it comes to the making of investments from Asian countries. Therefore, if you're not able to comprehend the language of your choice, the investment may prove to extremely risky without an Fundamental Analyzing Support and a well-studied plan to support it.

The design of an economy calendar is, therefore, one of the most important steps to manage your data collection activities. You can download the already-compiled calendars on the internet, but they must be upgraded and redesigned depending on the needs of your.

Once an appropriate calendar is established it is possible to study the different microeconomic and macroeconomic information that is available in each asset.

21

1.3.1 Data on macroeconomics

Macroeconomics is thought to be a part of finance which involves the study of a few basic measures in order to conduct a proper fundamental analysis.

In the first place, macroeconomics focuses on assessing the relationship between the national gross domestic product and debt in order to comprehend the development of a state.

The second is macroeconomics, which considers what the rate of employment in the country is. This number can be broken down by age as well as by season in order to conduct different research. It is one of the most important indicator of the Fundamental Analysis. The rate should be low to avoid loss of value to the money, however not too low , as states which has an inflation level that is close to zero could end in the midst of a recession. The macroeconomics section also deals with the rate of growth in the economy and demonstrates how much the country will benefit in the near future and meet certain goals.

Each of these ratios or rates can be used by an analyst to evaluate the direction of an economic scenario. But, macroeconomics doesn't mean individual actions as much as markets viewed as a system of aggregates. Thus, the analyst must be able to mix the outputs of each company to figure out the direction of economic growth in an asset might be. The analysis should be done based on raw data that is not processed by any other body or agencies.

There are a variety of reports available on the internet, that offer opinions on the trends in asset prices. But, these interpretations could be incorrect This is why it is crucial to trust the expertise of one's self instead of the reports provided by third entities. Additionally, these reports could be referring to time horizons that differ from those established by an analyst. This means that the interpretations could be different and based on totally different reasoning.

In this way it is important to break the trade down into two distinct parts that are the liquid capital which is represented by receipts and payments and delayed capital, which is comprised of investments, credit and loans. Additionally an analyst must look at the balance between national and international payments to determine whether exports are worth more than the value of imports.

But fundamental analysts are able to employ systems that make it easier to understand the data and provide a more realistic view of economic. Particularly there are two models that are able to perform the task well, specifically investment savings – Liquidity Cash which is known as IS-LM, and the Aggregate Demand Aggregate Demand, also commonly referred to as AD-AS. The first of these models is charged with determining which equilibrium point at an economic level and then using this to determine the point at which it is best to create forecasts for the medium time. The second model in contrast concentrates to the specific factors that lead the market to an equilibrium point, and attempts to determine why these events take place. But, it's not right to completely exclude from the analysis made by such models, the effects of fluctuations which are characteristic of the market over the short time. Indeed, these are essential in order to determine the direction of the market over a longer period of time.

Thus, the analysis of data from macroeconomics is essential in understanding the development of certain assets, or of the whole market for financial services, but in addition, it is essential to understand the wider economic reality. A study based on the data could yield unexpected results that can either confirm or disprove the results of microeconomic analyses, but that still provide important analysis to determine what the trend in the market could be over the long-term. Also, it considers unanticipated circumstances.

The benefit of Fundamental Analyzing macroeconomic data is shown by the possibility of effortlessly and at any moment receiving information and data related to the actual economic conditions observed.

1.3.2 - Microeconomics data

Microeconomics is distinct from macroeconomics because it examines the individual economic reality, and evaluates their development over time. Particularly, it is a study of changes in the market for individual individuals, which are understood as consumers of the goods and services of businesses and the services provided by them, as well as of private companies, playing the dual roles of suppliers and consumers as well as organizations as well as private and public institutions.

It is essential for the basic analyst to realize that macroeconomic statistics are not able to have a true value unless they are supported by microeconomic indicators. If a particular firm, however massive, sacks a portion staff members, the decision will not have any impact for macroeconomic information.

However when the cuts affect several businesses that means the rate of employment that is considered to be an economic quantity, will be affected by the variation in its value.

In any event it is always advisable to analyze and blend the information that is available so that you can be able to better understand the market's current trends are.

The primary analysts look at the data of microeconomics, based on an idea that lies at the heart of this system, which is the basis of what subjects undertake in each and every step in search of the possibility of earning. Therefore, every business sells an item in the marketplace at a cost which is more than the sum of individual costs involved in producing it. If this isn't the case then the business will be facing an expense and, in the world of microeconomics it is not acceptable. Companies that generate losses will eventually quit the market. After they have reached an amount that is certain that they will no longer be in a position to support the expenses. So investors will have to choose only ones that have a reasonable likelihood of profit in the long run as well as be careful not to make some investments on the basis of their own intuition.

This kind of temptation, which frequently leads to bankruptcy are often triggered by the delicate circumstances when traders are crossing their fingers. They've chosen the wrong company to trust their money and then attempt to rectify the mistake through increasing risk associated with their investment.

1.4 Operations-related difficulties when using the Fundamental Analysis

The issues that arise from the use of Fundamental Analysis mean that there are those who disdain it and prefer Technical Analysis. In reality, however it is this complexity that is one of the reasons why most of the people who do not apply this kind of analysis. If, you are using this type of analysis, in the Technical Analysis, it is sufficient to research the various indicators and learn about them, but in the Fundamental Analysis, it is vital to interpret the signals in light of the financial, economic as well as other variables which could be influencing a specific situation or market. The interpretation of this is operationally complicated as it is a step beyond logicand is difficult to control and not be influenced by emotion in favor of logic. Rumors can affect the price of goods and services.

Therefre, the analysis is the most difficult operational issue of Fundamental Analysis. It is the most difficult part of Fundamental Analysis, and becomes much more complicated because of the large amount of data that must be analysed that can be quantified in thousands of indicators which can impact positively or negatively impact the price. To solve this issue fundamental analysts attempt to limit the most important data in order to simplify at least some of the process of analysis.

Fundamental Analysis Fundamental Analysis focuses on the study of the macroeconomic as well as microeconomic reference environments built on an econometric model that can identify the interrelations between the studied economic realities. But the models aren't adaptable, and only when they are used in the decisions of economic policies made by the government. If they are utilized for financial markets, these models can't be easily adapted because they comprise variables that are not managed over time due to their particularity towards certain markets and not others. Additionally, because of the volume of data that needs that must be modified and the timeframe for each signal, they will not be accurate.

In this regard, it is crucial to possess an extensive understanding of mathematics and econometrics, as well as the market as well as a strong predisposition to the interpretation of data.

Company and sector analysis can be difficult to determine the various economic, financial and equity situations of businesses in order to calculate the income flows associated with equity in the most accurate manner. To accomplish this, investors who choose to put money into the market with Fundamental Analysis can use supports that are either free or cost-based with information that are different from the information provided by various brokers.

Many websites have been built all over the world to provide an important database for people who wish to conduct trading online with confidence like Financialweb However, in Europe the continent, there are no websites like this.

The understanding of financial analysis is a requirement to Fundamental Analysis, made starting with balance sheets for companies and market data, as well as the various appreciation indices However, brokers do not provide tools like this. Thus, the only way to properly apply the Fundamental Analysis is to become proficient fundamental analysts.

Chapter 2: Charts: Linear, Bar, Candlestick,

And Point-And-Figure Chart Patterns

Japanese candlestick trading began in Japan in the 18th century. It was a time when commodity traders making bets on the rice price. The popularity of the technique exploded during the West in the year 1991, when Steve Nison published his book "Japanese Candlestick Charting Techniques." Candlestick analysis is a method of predicting that is used to identify prices and changes in trends. Candlesticks display price movements over the time frame specified and are comprised of "bodies" along with "wicks." This is where you'll learn the fundamentals of understanding and reading the candlestick chart. Be aware that the analysis described below could differ from the traditional security or other theories due to the perpetual nature of many cryptocurrency markets. The patterns and formations are determined by my own interpretation of crypto-centric trading. It may be offensive to some traditionalists!

When you're reading about candlesticks it's important to comprehend the way that price action shapes the structure of them. Every candle can be described as an empty canvas which displays the value change in the given time period. For example, a one-hour (1H) candle displays the price movement over an hour. The candle has been formed after the completion one hour. A fresh one is formed on the next hour. The start of the new candle is the first transaction in the new period. If the candle will be colored green (buyer control) and colored red (seller managed) will be determined by cost of the asset in relation to the point at which it started during the period. For instance that Bitcoin has a price of $10,000 at the time that the candle starts (opens) and increases to $10,050 by the time it comes to an end (closes) then it will then be green. However, if Bitcoin falls below $10,000 within the time frame it will be red. "The "body" refers to the solid part of a candle, which marks its distance from the time of opening and closing of the period being studied. The more distance that is between the open and close points and close, the greater the size of the body.

If an asset appreciates in value but then decreases in value during the time of a candle's creation and it forms an wick. The the wick appears as thin lines indicating the low or high point at which the price was before it changed direction. So, when candles form wicks it is possible to observe a shift in the person who controls the value of the asset. Either buyers took control, but lost control later or sellers took control, but then lose the control later. Consider trading as a tug-of war in which sellers and buyers are always fighting to draw the opposing side on their side. It is important to note that many traders employ"shadow" or "shadow" to refer to the wick, while some may limit the definition for "wick" only to the top part of a candle. They may also use"tail" for the bottom "tail" to describe the bottom. This manual only employs"wick," and not "wick" and is applicable to all of the above purposes.

Exerpts from Trading View (Examples of two different kinds of candles Examples 1 with a smaller body that ends that has buyers taking control Example 2 that has a larger body that ends by putting sellers under control)

A trader might look at the chart in several time periods to learn the situation. For instance one could compare those candles in the charts of 1H to the chart for 4H to carefully analyze or dissect the price movement. In the case of example when the 4H chart shows a dominant seller candles, this might be helpful for traders to know when during those four hours, the sellers took over.

In the end, candlestick analysis involves studying the candlesticks' strings together. Knowing what each candle or sets (formations and patterns) are able to aid traders to determine the severity of a trend and when a trend is likely to reverse. A great analogy can be drawn from the world of flowers. Each flower is distinct and beautiful in its own right however when it is arranged together in a bouquet or a cluster its beauty and significance are amplified. Flowers can be placed endlessly to create various designs or trigger different emotions - red roses to express love, yellow daffodils for happiness, sunflowers to express happiness, tulips to convey well-wishes, or even a mixture of different flowers to look beautiful. Similar to a candlestick, it can be appreciated just for its idea as a stand-alone item, however when paired together with the other candles, its individual suggestion can be strengthened in friendship or completely create a new significance.

I warn that candlesticks are tools to be considered in the context of other elements of analysis. Consider, for instance, the consideration of the candles' surroundings trading volume charts, chart patterns, trend lines oscillators, momentum gauges such as the RSI or any other signals from the market.

Numerous forms are seen in consolidation, reversals as well as continuations, which is why it's important to know the other factors of the analysis of technology. I don't usually trade solely based on candlestick pattern without a related indicator.

Support and resistance lines for trend are also the foundation of chart pattern creation. Through applying the basic principles of trend lines, and then combining both resistance and support lines traders can detect patterns that could be used to predict future trends. Incredibly, a lot of easily identified patterns can be found across all markets, which allows traders to anticipate the direction of future price movements with a reasonable degree of accuracy. In the past traders have utilized the value of the statistical analysis of price action using patterns in chart that frequently occur and their importance to the way a market changes. Presently, "ChartLogic" offers the most thorough analysis of patterns on charts on the cryptocurrency markets.

Chart reading is an amazing thing. I'm not lying. Charting will not only aid in understanding any global market, when you watch the dips and swings on reports, but it also provides an unrivalled insight into the human psyche and actual trading of money between participants in the market. Charts are a historical account of capital flows and the collective psychology of a group on every chart, you will see the market movements that have ruined the lives of people. Charts record collective moments of fear or extreme greed as well as an opportunity to predict future price movements. Charts are useful tools and being an expert chartist is a process which often turns into an obsession.

What we're looking at when looking at charts will be the price of an asset in the course of time. It doesn't matter if it's stocks, cryptos or commodity or other type of asset, a technical chart can be defined by the the X and Y axes. The one axis, X is a measure of time. On the Y axis it's an indication of values or prices. We are therefore analyzing values that change in time.

A chart is constantly changing and needs to be reviewed in the course of its development. A specific aspect of a chart can alter as time passes. The traders should be prepared to change their dispositions when the price action alters. Charting doesn't have to prove the validity of a prior theory or to prove a disposition (although sure, many investors are fond of putting their own biases on assets through charts). Instead, it's about looking into possible outcomes that could be next from an objective, neutral viewpoint. There is a chance that you have a bias which is fine for a person however, as a trader the subjectivity and biases of traders pose an issue that could directly hinder your judgment and effective strategy for trading.

When selecting a chart for the specific asset, I choose one that represents information from an exchange, with at least years of history on the chart for the asset. For instance, when considering Bitcoin I use the chart of

"Coinbase," "Bitmex" (XBT) and "Binance" since the history of price is long and the liquidity of these exchanges is very high and the price movement isn't as often subject to the outliers that can occur in a volatile market. It is difficult to chart if you must account for the possibility of a "flash collapse" (a sudden increase or decrease in price that isn't the normal course of price movements). But, "Bitmex's" XBT still often suffers from extreme slide and must be handled with care.

Chapter 3: Wave Theory Of Ralph Nelson

Elliot

Ralph Nelson Elliot is an economist who created"the "wave theory." He believed that economic developments are cyclical , with the cyclical nature of optimism and despair.

These waves are a part of the cycle of three fundamental states: recession, depression and expansion.

Elliot predicted his theory that when the economic system goes to a depression and stays there until a sufficient amount of pessimism been built up to force it back to recession. In a recession your only option to escape is expansion (or release of pressures that have been accumulated).

Elliot believed that in order for the economy to be able to transition through those states, the economy needs to go through shorter cycles in the greater one. For instance, if you examine the greater depression wave to the

41

smaller ones, it is possible to observe how they are aligned.

Elliot's theory reveals a clear relationship between economic events as well as their timing. A wave-theory developed by Ralph Nelson Elliot is a fact that is indisputable.

When the economy is changing and people's opinions change, so do their beliefs regarding whether or not they have changed. These beliefs could be founded on any of a variety of sources, from personal observations to the news media, but they are constantly changing each when the economy is affected in any way.

Elliot's wave theory is evident in many areas of our society, from people buying during times of economic growth to flourishing to investors who purchase stocks at a bargain and then sell them once they're costly.

What is Wave Theory?

Wave theory by Ralph Nelson Elliot began developing in the early 1980s , when the U.S.

was going through an era of contraction and over-production. The country was in recession and Elliot believed that it was likely to continue into recession once again. Instead the economy was expected to last between five and one years and then rebound into an expansion phase, before falling into a new recession.

However, the scenario did not go as planned. Instead it continued to decrease until the end of July, 1981 at which point interest rates were increased by the Nixon administration's Federal Reserve Board to prevent inflation from exceeding 10%..

The economy recovered to expansion in April 1982. But, as the theory of wave was based on the idea that the economy would remain stuck in recession for between one to five times, Elliot had missed seeing the wave.

Pessimism and optimism are the basis of the cycle of economic growth and contraction. Elliott's wave theory deals with the psychological aspects of market. It's utilized to study the way people make assumptions about the future. These expectations guide their decisions to invest and buy according to how they feel (expectations).

This theory is based on analyzing the past trends in stock prices over the course of. Elliott predicted that economies would repeat a pattern or cycle that would last up to 55 years.

Essential Rules in Elliot's Wave Theory

Elliott's theory of waves is complicated and has several issues. The first is that it has its foundation in the notion that the economy is an unchanging cycle of ups and downs. But, this doesn't be applicable to all economies.

Another issue in Elliott's wave theory is that there are many complex dependencies that are hidden in the waves and cycles. This means that they're not easy to discern in the event that you don't know exactly what you're searching for.

It's a difficult concept to grasp. The theory is founded on the belief that markets exhibit powerful emotions, and those emotions trigger buyers and sellers to purchase stocks based on the mood of their buyers. The theory also attempts to show how the performance in an economic system can be determined through studying historical trends of the stock market in the course of time.

Elliott's Wave Theory Possible?

Other famous economists have expanded on Elliott's wave theory. For instance, in the year the year 1968 Frost and Prechter created an entirely new method for analyzing the wave theory dubbed "Frosted Prechter." It's an extremely complicated system that consists of up to 720 waves in greater cycles.

In the business world, there is plenty of truth in this notion. Businesses will prosper during times of growth, and prosper in times of recession, because they have constructed an enduring base in the period of expansion. When investing in stocks, overall is not easy as economic cycles are repeated frequently as well without warning.

The theory of economics known as the wave relies on the notion that economics follow a pattern of downs and ups. But there are instances where the economy grows in a way that is different from its size, such as the growth of the economy of North America since 1975, that was significantly higher than its share of global growth, which was 10 10%.

There are many debates that exist about this idea in the present. While it is generally believed that the economic system goes through contraction and expansion phases throughout time, it has yet to be established the extent to which it is an established cycle.

Elliot Wave Types

The five kinds of waves that Elliott describes in his wave theory are diagonal, impulse flat, correction and triangle.

* Impulse Waves They generally have three wave structure (either ABC or ABA). This is by

far the most long of the waves , and is made up of impulse waves that move in a single direction.

Diagonal Waves waves are five-wave patterns (ABCDE) which have ascending highs, and lows that are rising.

The Flat Waves possess four-wave structure (ABCDE) that have rising highs, and low-rising bottoms.

The Correction waveforms have 5 wave structures (AABA or WXYZ) and could be horizontal or diagonal.

* Triangle Waves waves are composed of five-wave patterns (ABCDE) with rising lows and rising highs.

Elliot Wave Cycle

Sometimes the wave theory behind Elliott's wave cycle is likely to be false. However, we can see patterns in the cycles that are linked to significant events, such as economic and political changes. We can utilize those data to determine what markets might be expected to shift.

Elliott's cycle of waves consists consisting of 3 primary waves as well as 3 primary subdivisions: Primary Intermediate as well as secondary wave. Primary waves are typically an extremely large one that increases in strength as it moves towards completeness.

The intermediate wave is typically between an impulse and the correction wave. It is generally the most compact of the three and always falls within the ABC pattern.

The second wave is in between the impulse and a correction wave. It's typically more extensive than an intermediate one, however it is less than an impulse.

Elliott Wave Theory - The Bottom Line

Certain investors rely on the theory of the wave in economics to determine where the markets will move in the future. It is crucial to keep in mind that this theory is extremely complex and not always correct. It is nevertheless helpful in providing a common sense method of making investment decisions and analysing historical stock prices in relation to time.

Chapter 4: The Theory Of William Delbert

Gann

William Delbert Gann's theories have provided a few basic market strategies But let's get into more of the technical aspects. The majority of traders utilize price charts for analyzing the performance of stocks. They are referred to as "technical analysis" tools.

There are a variety of charts. The two most commonly used are bar charts or line graphs. Bar charts depict every day's data as a rectangle with the opening and closing prices, as well as high, low and closing prices on the bottom and top of the rectangular. Line graphs illustrate the way in which a stock's price fluctuates over time, displaying the fluctuations and changes during a particular time.

There are some fundamental principles in technical analysis. Certain of these principles were first discovered in the work of William

Delbert Gann, and others were discovered by traders who used Gann's techniques.

Another rule in technical analysis is that if a share starts falling, that's typically a good indication it is likely to continue falling. As mentioned earlier, this could be considered to be an early warning signal.

A third principle of analysis states you should follow the trends regardless of how long it continues. That means that if a market is constantly moving higher and up, you should continue to buy it until the trend ends, then sell it (or sell it short). But if you're wrong and the price isn't able to keep going up but it isn't the end of the story.

A fourth principle of analysis in the field is that if a share starts increasing, that is typically a good sign that it is likely to continue rising. This could be considered to be an early warning signal.

Let's discuss the most powerful concepts (traders) that is RSI (Relative Strength Index). The late Mr. Gann taught that price tends to fluctuate in relation to the most recent price changes. Thus, as long as there is an orderly and steady trend in large volume, then it is advisable to utilize the measure of relative strength to predict the direction prices are likely to take in the future.

Chapter 5: Supports And Resistances

A Support Zone (or Level) or Support Zone

A support zone can be described as an area in which the price is subject to a lot of buying pressure. Professional traders are patiently waiting for the bullish confirmation of price action signal to place their massive orders along the key markets' support zones.

A Resistance Zone is also known as a Level.

The market's resistance zone is where the bulls exhaust themselves and the sellers dominate the market. The most skilled traders use this confirmation sign of bearish price movement in order to complete their short-term trades at a level of resistance.

How do you draw the perfect Resistance Level or Support Level?

We only require two connecting points to create the main support or resistance level in this market. Professional traders make use of the latest lows of the market to determine an acceptable support level. To find the most important resistance level, they take the recent highs, and then join them by drawing the horizontal line. Let's look at an example:

The Market has Support Levels and Resistance Levels

From the above picture In the above image, the two points are utilized to define the main support level for the market. The points 3 and 4 represent the potential buying zones for traders. Contrarily the points "a" along with "b" represent the two highest levels that have been which are the primary resistance zone for the market. How do we trade at this area? Do we need to simply place buy orders at the support level and sell when we reach resistance? The answer is no.

The importance of moving averages and how to use them to buy stocks

A moving average (or Moving Average) is basic special examination tool that aids in determining the direction of price through the analysis of an average of prices. Investors can choose to take an average of any period between 10 minutes and seven months , or even longer durations. There are a variety of advantages to moving averages and investors can utilize different kinds of these.

Candlestick Charts

When you are trying to make an accurate price chart you should take a handful of different elements of data. In the beginning, you'll need to look at the price the particular stock began the day with, the price which it topped at (you must also determine its lowest level) then, what was the price at which it closed. The data is displayed as an unbroken box that is pierced by a line once you input the data into the platform you're using. The points on that line represent the price of the high and low as well as the outer and topmost edges of the box indicate the closing and opening price. Stocks that finished higher than when they started are colored one color. Stocks that closed lower than when they started are then colored with a different color.

Candlestick Form

The container created is typically known as a candlestick and it can do more than simply provide details about what happened over the years. It could also make it easier to figure out what's likely to take place in the near future.

Range

The range of the candlesticks represents the level of volatility that the markets are experiencing. The greater the volatility the less reliable the potential for your base assets to be in comparison to previous averages. It is possible to assess the volatility of the market by comparing the length of the line in relation to the overall dimensions that the entire box. If the market's volatility is high, this box is huge and the line will be tiny. If the volatility currently has been low, then the reverse is likely to be the case.

Split Line

Once you've got a good grasp of the range as well as the body, you'll need to turn your focus to the upper portion of the range. The line's upper portion is then capped at the top of the day's prices but at the same marking the point at which supply again began to surpass demand, leading to an overall reduction in value. Thus, the top spot is the tension that the stock endured in the specified time period. The lower part of the line will provide similar details, except about the lowest point for the day and the moment where demand started to surpass supply.

Dual Price Bars

If you decide to add another value bar into the study you're conducting You will be in a position to utilize two price bars to serve as a benchmark. This gives you an notion of the amount of change that the market is experiencing within a more concrete way than only looking at one bar. A second bar can let you more quickly decide if what you observed in the first bar was an error or something that can be taken action on enough to take action earlier sooner rather than later. In the end, you'll be able to use this method when you have to figure out the extent of a bar or, as the case may be an average bar or any other type of comparison, too. This will help you comprehend the price process in a much more specific manner and increase the effectiveness of your analysis than it could be.

Hook Reversal

Hook reversals are a candlestick pattern that appears in the smaller time frame charts. They are able to appear on uptrends and downtrends and are useful in forecasting a setback in the current trend. This pattern is reminiscent of an engulfing candle, but with an elevated low and lower high when compared to the candlestick from the previous day. This is an unusual design, since the of the difference between the first and second bars' bodies is small when compared to other patterns that engulf.

If the pattern is identified in an uptrend, the opening will usually be close to the previous high, and the low will be close to the lower low. Additionally this pattern is typically connected to other harami positions since the second candle's body is created inside the body of the first candle.

Abandoned Baby

Another candlestick pattern that can be useful in assessing the likelihood of an upcoming setback to the current trend. This pattern is formed by a set of candles that have distinct features. One bar is a candlestick in red which is massive and clearly visible in the context of a prior downward trend. Second bar is expected to open with an open that is equal to the closing gaps below the bottom in the bar before it. In the final, there will be huge white candlestick which opens higher than the first bar. The bar is also a sign of changing sentiments of traders.

This is a fairly uncommon pattern, however it's reliable in forecasting a shift in the predominant downtrend. The reliability of the signal is further increased when combined with other technical indicators like RSI or MACD.

Bearish Baby Abandoned

This pattern of candlesticks is helpful to signal a reversal of an uptrend that is currently in place. It's also a triangular pattern. The first bar comprises a single white candlestick, which is huge and located within an earlier uptrend that was clearly defined. Second bar identical to the one found in the bullish baby. The last bar is a red candle which is big and will be open underneath another bar. It's also helpful for understanding the current mood of the trader.

Chapter 6: Charles Dow's Tide Theory And Subdivision Of Trends (Major Medium, Major And Minor)

Charles Dow started as a journalist, but will be remembered forever as one the founders in technical analysis. Dow was born in Sterling, Connecticut, on the 6th of November 1851. He was the child of a farmer, who became journalist when he was 21 in close proximity to Massachusetts working for The Springfield Daily Republican. There Dow met the editor of his company, George W. Danielson, the editor. He was so impressed by Dow's meticulous research and reporting that he requested Dow to join the group composed of Wall Street financiers on their excursion to Colorado to look at options for investing in mining in silver.

Dow was a sharp and a lively young man who earned the investors' trust during the trip, and invited investors to discuss with him the information that was helpful and what information was not suitable for Wall Street investors. It was a brief four-day journey however, Dow gained a valuable lesson: Information, or the most reliable information, is what transforms an investment risky into a multimillion-dollar return. Following the trip in 1880, and at 29 years old, Dow moved to New York and became a member of his first job at the "Kiernan Wall Street Financial News Bureau" as reporter. Dow was now able to find valuable information and observe its impact on the value of the stock.

Two years later, and aged 31 years old, Dow joined forces with his long-time companion as well as Brown university dropout Edward Davis Jones, to create the "Dow Jones & Company" Financial news agency that published a two-page financial daily news summary for the following 7 years. In 1889 the new firm launched a fully-fledged paper and dubbed it"Wall Street Journal. "Wall Street Journal." It is the Wall Street Journal we read every day. Seven years later in 1896"the "Dow Jones Industrial Average"

(DJIA) was established and consisted of the from the prices at which closing occurred for 12 businesses divided by 12 to create an average.

The Dow taught us of market changes (up and down) and also that they can be forecast by looking at indexes or the average price of a set of companies that reflect the economic system. Dow considered that the industrials (the DJIA) and railroad transportation (the index was developed the following year around the year 1897) were the main motors of our economy and if they were not working, the economy would fail and the reverse was true. Of of course, this isn't always the case, particularly with railroad transportation, which is considered to be as the main engine of the economy. However, the idea of signaling is still in place. That means that if it is true that Dow Jones Industrial Average (DJIA) was created by him is falling and news anchors across the globe are able to start spreading "news" that the "market is falling," and this could affect the behaviour of investors who are cautious and causes the industrials market to decline.

Dow Theory Dow Theory

Dow theorem is an concept of price movements built on 255 editorials Charles Dow wrote in the Wall Street Journal. When he passed away in 1902, the theory went through numerous updates to remain relevant. The concepts of Dow theory Dow concept have been repeated repeatedly throughout the last century, though with slightly different timelines and focusing on the most significant concepts.

The most important thing to do is know the concept Dow realized: There appears to be a pattern that repeats in the world of humans making investments in stock. Our behavior as a species hasn't altered over long which is why these patterns are likely to remain in place for the rest of time. Be aware of this fundamental fact that you'll be in a position to choose what aspects that comprise Dow theory you believe in. Dow theory you trust.

My belief is Dow was right in his assumption that the existence of a pattern. The time-frame of the patterns might or might not be a small amount off, and some traders, like Gann and Gann, have observed more complex patterns. I don't want you remember how long a bull period is since that would cause you to believe the information as true and you will not be able to recognize human behavior. However, repeated behavior can be different depending on the economic, political, or even environmental situations. It is possible to begin noticing patterns when you've gained experience however, only if you are searching for new patterns.

The six Tenants in the Dow Theory. Dow Theory

The following are the main ones markets follow several cycles simultaneously. The first is that markets follow an ongoing primary which is referred to as a major trend either bearish or bullish. Then comes the medium-term secondary reaction which is retracing 1/3 to 2/3 (33%-67 percent of the previous price. It could be in any direction, either bearish or bullish. It is followed by small or a brief movements that trace the price of the stock in a lesser degree. It is possible to imagine that the market would exhibit an extended bullish trend that lasted between March 2009 and 2017 with a medium change in 2016 and 2015, and several short swings on the course. This is an extremely insightful observation. It is possible to see many trends when zooming in and zooming out on the Dow Jones price chart.

DJIA Sharpening and Smoothing of Long-Term Trends

A further extension of the initial principle that is part of The Dow Theory is that not only do we notice various patterns for short and long-term according to how long or short of a time frame we choose to focus on, but there are other patterns when we alter the time interval between the data we collect. You can analyze any time period by with any interval ranging from one minute to a year. The longer interval of 4 hours is an example. It eliminates the various shorter-term trends that are evident in the chart of 1-hour intervals.

Our indicators of these patterns may not be right. Although humans behave similarly in response to the same stimuli the stimuli that are in the environment are comparable but not the same as the previous times. If you don't understand read it over again until you can understand. In addition, when we alter the interval of time from a longer interval to shorter intervals it is possible to see an unobserved pattern that we did not see before OR increase the amount of statistical noise. This is another way to say that we can obscure patterns we observed within the longer time interval.

The choice of the intervals is based on knowledge However, I'll make it easier. Consider that it takes between 10 and 20 intervals or data points to get an identifiable pattern to be evident to inform you if you should sell or buy. If we select a one-minute interval, as day traders usually do and we receive signals each 10-20 minutes. However I run many businesses I have to be aware of and I can only trade once per daily or even every few days. To suit my needs I utilize the 4-hour 12 hour, 24-hour, and 4-hour intervals. This allows me to have the option of a few days or several weeks between trading, and it is a good fit for my needs.

Chapter 7: What Types Of Trend Lines Are

And How They Are Made

It is not enough to discuss the upward and downward trend without showing you ways to draw trends. They aren't difficult to create and they are among the most straightforward of the analytical tools that you can encounter in Forex. When used in the right way they is a good one for trading. For novice traders using trend lines, they are the best analysis tool you employ. If possible, mix them with other tools you can use.

To draw lines of trend, identify the location and link the three or two important tops or bottoms in price movements. In order for a trend to be established, it must have an intersection of two points with a third line in order to verify the direction of the movement. If drawing an upward direction, the trend line should join into the lowest (trough) and support (trough) points, whereas when it is a downward trend the line should connect with the highest line of resistance. This is called the top.

Classic Chart Patterns

The patterns of the chart show the dominant mental state that is underlying the market's price at any time. Knowing the dominant sentiment that is driving the market lets traders take advantage of the most lucrative trading opportunities when they come up. So, they'll be able to follow the trend , and avoid the error to "bucking with the market trend."

We also know that when prices fluctuate between one and another based on the changing mood of the market participants during any particular session, they create distinct and distinct designs on charts. These patterns reflect the general market mood that has taken over of the market over the various trading times. This is why it is crucial to examine these various chart patterns since they have enormous predictive value and provide us with a hint of which direction prices will be to go.

Technical analysts and market technicians have observed for a long time that, when given the similar market conditions and identical resources available, investors are more likely be able to respond and act in nearly exactly the same way they have before. It's like it's a cycle of history that repeats itself. This is the reason why there is the classic chart patterns their predictive power. This is precisely the kind of thing we want to see in a price chart, familiar patterns that help us determine what direction the market will take following past market movements.

There may not be any scientific reason for this phenomenon. Yet, this phenomenon has been noticed often, not only in the stock market, but other financial markets too. This is the main reason we look into chart patterns in order to make the most of trading opportunities that come with these patterns. They are either indicative in the direction of current trends, or reverse, giving us an idea of the best way to setup our trading strategies accordingly. The traditional chart patterns don't show up often, but if they occur, you can be certain it will follow the same course of action that it did previously.

Chapter 8: Gaps

Gaps are the areas of the chart in which there is a major change but no trading between. The stock could have was higher or lower in relation to where it ended the previous day. As the name suggests there is a gap on the chart.

As I've mentioned it happens due to abrupt changes in an increase in earnings for a company or announcements that trigger a swift reaction. In the case of an influx of buyers when there is a surge in interest, investors will raise their bids and create gaps and the stocks eventually go higher. In the same way, a lot of selling pressure causes sellers to lower their prices in order to create an increase in gap due to the desire to sell their holdings.

These gaps typically occur during trading days. As an example, a share may be trading at $150 by a Monday, and then open it could open with $145 the following Tuesday. Because they happen in the middle of the day, it is best to look at them on an daily or hourly charts. However, you'll be able to trade it on shorter-term time frames such as five-minute charts.

JP Morgan's Share on the hourly chart

The JP Morgan stock initially closed at around $155.75 in April 8,, before closing lower and opening at around $154 the following day. The following day, that same day, on the 9th April JP Morgan's stock was trading at around $155.25 prior to eventually gapping higher when it opened at around $155.75 the following day. This means that, as you observe, gaps are quite frequent between trading days.

The reason that gaps are effective is due to the fact that stocks love to fill gaps. This is why these levels become the benchmarks for algorithms and traders to revisit. This, in turn, implies that they could be important levels of resistance and support that you may not have anticipated.

Bullish Gaps

The bullish gap occurs when a stock is increased its gap. It means that the stock traded higher than the level it was closing the previous day. To make money from an upward gap, what you're looking for is for the price to slide back, then fill in that gap and turn it into a support. If this happens and the stock reverses following or any of the reverses we've discussed about, that's an indication of bullishness to go into the market and purchase. In simplest words, gaps are possible areas that can be transformed into support or resistance.

Apple's Shares on the Hourly Chart

In this case the Apple stock has formed the shape of a geometric triangle. However, prior to its creation, the stock increased from $127.50 up to $128.50 on the 4th of May. It filled in the gap by retracing back to the level , and then formed an upward-facing double bottom. While symmetrical triangles can be either direction however, they are symmetrical in nature. Bullish gap-fill is incredibly bullish. It eventually broke higher, breaking above the previous low, then then ended in running to the high of the swing triangle, where one can look at taking a profits.

Its stock on the five-minute chart

This illustration shows how it is possible to trade gaps in shorter-term time frames. In this case, NIO's stock was able to gap up, but then it retracted lower to transform that low into support. After that, it surged higher over that "9 EMA" and its resistance level was about $37.90--simple "gap to go."

The Stock of Bank of America on the hourly Chart

One thing you must remember is that gaps won't always be filled in the following day. They may also be filled in a few days or even a few weeks prior to the time they first formed. While this isn't common however, it's feasible. This is why it's a good habit to continuously monitor possible levels of support to spot any gaps the stock is getting close to.

This illustration shows how BAC's shares filled the gap and gained the support it needed a few days after it jumped higher. Although it briefly broke beneath the gaps, the stock remained at the level and even created the long-legged "doji" which indicates the possibility of a trend reverse higher. The stock went on to form an overhanging candle, which broke above the 9 EMA and then immediately faced resistance in the following candle. The following morning, it remained to hold its 9 EMA and was able to break above a crucial resistance level about $41.10 to give another entry opportunity.

Apple's stock on the hourly chart

Another important thing to remember is that gaps don't have to be completely filled. The gap in Apple's shares jumped up from around $117 to around $118.20 but never came close to completely filling it. Even as the date is the 8th of March the gap hasn't been completely filled. But it could be used as a point of reference for buyers to increase their purchases in the event that the stock fills the gap. However, the most important thing to remember is the fact that the strategy of a gap, though extremely profitable, doesn't always succeed.

Facebook's Stock on an Hourly Chart

This is a great illustration of a failed gap fill. Facebook's stock rose but was unable to hold that level or transform it into support. It was instead not able to surpass the 9 EMA and then continued to fall. Therefore, be patient and watch for the appropriate signals!

Bearish Gaps

The bearish gap is the opposite. In these cases the gap in a stock is lower, which means that it started lower than it closed earlier. This is why stocks can turn into areas of resistance. What you should to see is how a particular stock reacts in the event that it fills those gaps. If it transforms into resistance and then reverses lower, it is an indication of a bearish gap and a chance to sell.

Apple's stock on the hourly chart

Apple's stock during this time fell from $126.35 down to $124.70 the following day. That day, it surged higher, filled in gaps, however it was unable to surpass. Instead, it erupted into a number of bearish gravestones as well as long-legged dojis which led to a break over the next few days.

Park Hotels and Resorts Stock on the hourly Chart

In this case the stock of PK was dropped lower, but it was unable to get past the gap after filling it. Instead it turned this gap in to resistance, and fell just below 9 EMA to confirm the reverse lower. This is where you should start your first short position that you can swing trade as there is no immediate resistance to be found. An important note: the trend line at the bottom of the chart isn't an indicator of support, but more of a place to observe the gap. The next day, the price verified that 9 EMA as resistance , and then dipped to fall further for a possible four-five percent gain.

The Stock of DoorDash in the 5 Minute Chart

DASH's stock fell from the previous day, but was able to fill that gap. If you are a trader, you must be looking out for an eventual reversal and looking for bearish signals. One such signal is it was overbought according to its RSI and also had the "bearish divergence." The stock discovered resistance in the gap, and then broke beneath the 9 EMA at which point you could begin a short position. Following that, it remained lower, made a tiny attempt to move higher, but failed, then formed an doji of gravestones, and then continued to fall. That's the second entry point.

Roku's stock on the hourly chart

Roku's stock, as in this instance, slid lower however, instead of turning into resistance, it smashed over it in the form of the bullish engulfing candle. This is why, as we've said that gaps aren't always played out. They're just different levels that can serve as a source of support or resistance which you must be aware of. If you spot a stock filling in a gap but confronting resistance, you must be expecting a reversal only to the negative.

There's no way to determine if a stock will turn 100% of gaps into resistance or support which is why confirmation is crucial. What you need to know is the reaction of stocks to these gaps and rememberthat gaps higher tend to transform into support, while gaps lower are generally resistance.

Chapter 9: Breakouts

They were a part of technical analysis quite a long time long time ago. They are defined as breakouts of trends within any asset type, like an increase in the volume of trading or a change in price from buying lower to selling higher. An investor's breakouts strategy is comprised of an entry strategy and exit strategy to capitalize on the trade made by market conditions and to avoid losses. Finding such trades through analyzing historical information and looking at markets to pinpoint zones of distinction between sellers and buyers.

Technical analysis should be utilized together with other tools to help with security selection and the management of portfolios, risk management and diversification. It also offers information to help you determine the best time to close and open positions.

The principle of the technical approach is to look at that the markets are a set of fluctuations (up as well as downward) as well as tendencies (uptrends or downtrends) that can be observed by those who trade on the market. This covers both longer-term trends as well as the short-term tendencies that can be observed in any given market or in a particular asset class.

The process of technical analysis is founded on the identification of patterns and trends that are observed throughout time. Using price charts to determine crucial points, peaks and valleys in those trend lines, and making use of these important times to predict future price fluctuations. The concept is straightforward It is that the market moves in the direction in a direction that the majority of investors are more likely to buy or sell due to their shift in mood. So, when the majority of investors are moving in a particular manner, prices rise as a large majority of investors are moving differently then the price drops.

The analysis of technical data can provide forecasts of the future of activity (and as a result the future price) by finding patterns and trends that aren't obvious to the untrained eyes. Line charts, for instance, frequently do this, as do other visual representations overlay historical data on live feeds of data or share prices in long-term time frames. These visualizations are then used to determine "signals," such as potential trends or patterns that might manifest when certain conditions occur.

The primary benefit of the process of technical analysis is that it will help investors understand the price they are being given for investment and not what they're willing spend for it. This is advantageous because the market usually outpaces the rate of growth in the value of shares, while undervaluing companies over the amount they're worth.

But, it doesn't attempt to predict the future but instead it analyzes previous price movements and determines what past events could impact future prices. This is why, technical analysis can be used to determine when to begin and stop trades by looking at these past events (and taking into account other factors such as volume).

Chapter 10: Fibonacci Retracement Levels

How do you draw Fibonacci Retracements Correctly?

This article will describe the steps needed to draw Fibonacci Retracement levels (or fibs) correctly. Additionally I will outline important characteristics that can increase the accuracy in the drawings you make. The procedure is simple and usually quick after you've had some practice. Even if you've had a lot of previous experience, there have a good likelihood of learning something new. Let's now go through the steps by providing explanations and diagrams to illustrate the process through real-world diagrams.

1. Discover the clearly distinct swing low and high. These are the points at which price shifted during the previous.

2. Create your Fib using the two points. In most charting software you simply click and hold the initial point. Here is the swing high , 286.63. Then , drag your mouse downwards

to align your fib to the other swing/reversal point. Here's the swing low of 252.92.

Then, you're done. As simple as that, you've had your lie drawn. However it's not over but not however. In the next section, I'll take you beyond the first steps that only a few people are taught and use because the majority of learning resources do not provide a lot of depth. This is why step 3 introduces lesser-known elements of drawing a properly drawn fib.

3. Confirm/validate your fib by using what I call a "confirmation/validation triangle." A confirmation or validation triangle is a triangle you can draw within your fib to confirm its validity and determine how far into the future it will remain reliable. Here's a two-part method of creating a validation triangle.

Check first that the levels of your fib are correct by checking whether they match with levels of resistance and support which have been established over time. If you notice price turning around or even stalling at the levels that are indicated in the fib. If price is able to move past the fib levels, it typically occur on greater volume or with a higher amount of normal price fluctuations. If you're viewing chart of commodity or currency that are not crowded, look for bigger movements in price that are breaking past fib levels. Then draw an arc of diagonal lines, often referred to"trend line," or "trend line" beginning from the place you started creating your Fib. The majority of charting software programs make this diagonal line show up in the fib automatically. In this instance this case, it's the high point which is 286.63. The trend line should be lined up with at minimum one point of swing in between swing's high and the swing low. In this case, the trend line may cross two reversal points in between both the low of swing and the swing high, where the fib's beginning and closes at.

Then, line up the end of the trend line with the line where your Fib ended (in this case it's that the swing high reversal level at 252.92). This creates a triangle in which you can observe previous resistance and support that validate and confirm the fib's value to you in the near future. I have added this gray triangle to illustrate the purpose. Most charting software only has the diagonal line, and don't shade or color the triangle. In any event the triangle is seen without or with color-coded in shades or colors. The trend line simply has to be in the general areas of the reversals that were observed in between swing highs and the swing low that the fib began and ended.

Be aware that the goal of fibs is to pinpoint important price levels that could offer resistance and support in the near future. Then, you can utilize these levels to better aid in determining your exit and entry strategies. We can see that the levels of resistance and support were correctly identified prior to the future price movement.

The trend line isn't essential, but I've discovered that it significantly increases the accuracy of fibs due to various reasons. The first is that the trend line is able to show and define the future zones of resistance and support as well as an approximate time when they'll take place. In the first instance it is not apparent because the price that is to come in the future did not touch the line of trend. Do not worry about it; there will be more examples in the future where the trend line in the confirmation triangle is supported and impedes price.

Effective Time-Range

Another reason why trend lines are beneficial in fibs is because of the "added contextual." The phrase I use in this is "effective timing range" for the fib. The effective range is the time period during which that a fib is the most reliable by the line drawn by the trend in the fib. The most reliable time period for a fib is determined by the distance further ahead the line of trend is until it converges with the second low/high of the swing which is the final part of the fib.

To make it clearer For greater clarity, let's review another example of the steps involved in drawing and validating an FBI. This time, it's an uptrend fib. Pay attention at the direction line as well as the effective time span.

1. You should be able to identify an easily identified swing low and a clearly defined swing high. These are the points at which price shifted over time. In this instance we can take advantage of the downtrend that started at the 32-dollar level however, here I will show an example using an uptrend.

2. Draw your fib by clicking on the swing low located at 22.73 points along the line. Drag your mouse until you align with the other swing/reversal point. Here is the swing high of 29.46. Note that 29.46 is an acceptable swing point since it is a reversal level (a low that is a swing). While it's not as established as the other places, such as 26.09 or 26.89 It is one of the points where price moved in the direction of the upward trend which began with the reversal low of 22.73.

3. Confirm or validate by drawing a confirmation triangle.

Are the levels of fib align with areas in which price stalled, reversed, or broke out in huge price movements or large volumes? Yes and you can check the pattern here:

1. Draw a diagonal line or a trend line, whatever you prefer. Begin with the point that you started making your fib with and in this instance is the high of the swing at 22.73.

2. Then, line across the trend line until meet at least one reverse point between the beginning and the end for the fib. We have 3.

3. Then, line up the final point in the line to the second line that finishes your fib range. in this instance it's the reversal top of the trend line at 29.46. You now have a valid fib that is confirmed using multiple methods to validate. In contrast to the previous example, that showed the chart hitting new heights, this chart includes more price action take a look back to the past.

4. To verify your levels of the fib for additional validity, compare them to prices from the past before the fib was initiated just expand

the line of the fib on the left. That means that you draw lines for past prices on one side. Make sure that your charting is able to extend level levels of fib to your left meaning you don't have to draw lines on your left.

Chapter 11: Technical Trend Indices (Moving Averages Macd, Rsi Obv, Bottom Line Etc.)

What makes anyone choose to "trade the trend"? We've all heard marketing pitches that claim that the market has been able to average a 10% annual return over the last 70 years, 80 years or whatever. Yes, it has. Take a look at a chart of the last 60 or 70 years and you'll discern. Why invest in the trend when you only need to do is purchase and then forget.

It's simple. If you'd invested in high-quality investments 50 to 60 years ago, and kept them for long time that means you'd be a self-made millionaire. For instance, if you didn't purchase and keep Edison Records, TWA, UAL, Bethlehem Steel, Enron or Polaroid. If you don't stay away from these firms and thousands of other ones that were into bankruptcy, you could become too old be able to enjoy your wealth, and have one foot on the ground or even be there. Therefore, rest easy and go to sleep; your descendants will be very grateful should you be fortunate enough fifty years ago to make smart investment choices.

Investment companies and their ever-growing sales staff constantly encourage the investor to buy and keep. The idea is easy, particularly when you consider that the most common retirement planning scenarios are all about simply adds a few eggs to an egg basket, and then twenty years after, a farm for chickens will magically pop up.

Buy and hold

While theoretically sound and well-intentioned, the Buy-and-Hold strategy is extremely difficult for investors to use. Why? It's a bit like saying to someone that the best way to get between Los Angeles to New York is to place one foot on top of another until they reach. There is no doubt about the directions, but can anyone follow them? The formula is missing the most important details.

For example, in a long-term bull market, such as that of 1982 until 2000, the buy-and hold strategy performed well. But during long-term trading range markets, it does not. The basic idea behind buy-and hold is that when investors attempt to make a move into and out of markets typically they purchase at the top and then sell at the lowest. This is especially true when an investor is not equipped with knowledge of the market and does not have a strategy for investing and trading.

However, a prudent investor will have issues when it comes to buy and hold, because they're aware of the risks of keeping a watchful eye on what happens. Although it's as simple as many people selling investment products wish it to be however, it's actually not so easy. Why? It is because history repeats itself. It is evident when you take a closer study of the history of markets.

When looking at the chart that shows the Dow Jones Industrial Average for the last 100 years looking from a bird's-eye perspective one of the thoughts that pops up to mind is "Just purchase and hold and eventually, you'll earn money." While many would wish to convince you that is the case, that's not always the scenario. Check out the chart of 1900 to 2008:

The chart above is extremely informative. While the market has risen for over 100 years there have been also long periods when it did not. Investors who invested in 1929 waited for 25 years to make a profit. The market was not trading higher than the 1929 highs till the late 1950s. Investors who invested in 1964 waited for 18 years to earn a profit, all the and then watched their investments plummet through several bear markets in the 18 years. They hoped that they could one day get back to breaking even. What happens to investors who bought in the year 2000 or 2007? What is the likelihood that they will make a profit! Thus, buy and hold is not as easy as it sounds.

Although the general movement has been rising for over 100 years, our typical life span is shorter than and our highest income and investing years are only a tiny fraction of one century. Some other important information about the history of markets include:

Financial advisors display a chart that states that the market is always up, suggesting that all you need to do is purchase and hold, and then eventually, you'll earn profits. It's nonsense.

In the chart, each longer-term increase is an "secular bull market" and any long-term decline or decline is an "secular bear market." The one has always been in line with the other.

The extended period of growth between 1982 and 2000 isn't a typical market trend. It is true that the market's long-term growth ending in the year 2000 isn't typical. Particularly since the only other time in over 100 years when the market experienced an eruptive advance was prior to it crashed in 1929.

However, many of the financial planners and advisors of today do not have a thorough understanding of market history , and they continue to provide advice to clients based on the false assumption that the era (1982-2000) would be normal. The most convincing explanation for the dramatic market growth between 1982 and 2000 is the income and investing times of the baby-boomer generation. Check out the population versus stocks chart below:

A variety of factors were involved in this development including the Internet and other emerging technologies that have opened up the market for online trading and other forms of trading. But, technological advancements aren't something that is new.

In the last 100 years, we've witnessed anything from AM radio television to spaceships. But, in those days of innovative inventions and new products that were introduced to the general public and the market was able to stick to the old patterns. This meant that the long-term bull and bear markets continued to exist, and the advancements remained normal and systematic.

The connection between the growth in the S&P 500 and the rise of baby boomers tells a story. The baby boomers reached their highest earnings years and began investing for retirement, the massive market surge followed closely. One could reasonably conclude that these investors are beginning to take cash out and will continue taking money from the market to fund their retirement. Thus I would be shocked to see another shift like this (1982-2000) in my lifetime.

Market history also shows us that market corrections of major magnitude as well as bear markets, occur more frequently than many believe. The issue is that the majority of investors don't plan to for the next correction, look forward to the time it will arrive, or even remember the destruction of the previous one. Thus, claiming that it will never be repeated doesn't ensure that it won't happen again. The quote is, "Those who do not take lessons from the past are likely to repeat the mistakes of their past."

Technical Momentum Indicators

Momentum indicators are designed to replace the eyeballing chart, by providing something more mathematical and scientific. They evaluate prices in the present with prices from the past to demonstrate how much the price is moving. It is possible to use momentum indicators like a speedometer. How quickly is the price moving? The fundamental calculation can be described as: "Momentum = closing price today/closing price x days earlier," and sometimes that's multiplied by 100, giving the percentage. It's simple, but you're unlikely to attempt it because we'll admit it "StockCharts'" or "Ameritrade's" data banks are able to perform the calculation a lot quicker than you.

For example that last week the stock was trading at $50. It's now upwards to $75. The momentum is: 75/50x100 =150 percent (or 1.5 for certain indexes). If the stock price last week was $50, and today it's trading at $25, the momentum is 25/50x100 = 50 percent or

0.5. You might have guessed that however, if the price is not changing and the index is 0.5, it will provide you with one or 100 percent.

Momentum indicators rarely provide signals, but they can be useful as confirmation of your trading strategies. In this case, for instance, you could verify a breakout when the momentum indicator is moving between the 98-99% area towards 101% 102%. The momentum has changed, which is, the price has changed direction. If it continues to rise and increasing, this means that your breakout will continue. Therefore, you can use these to reduce the amount of trades that are breakout-related that are canceled because they are found to be fake-outs and boost your winnings significantly.

Momentum indicators are also fascinating when they indicate divergence. If a price of a stock is still rising however the momentum indicator suggests that it's taking the brakes off it, that's a warning signal. It's similar to a train slowing down, which is usually a sign that there's a train coming up! If the price of the shares is still falling however that momentum gauge is turning back to 100%, then the momentum that caused the decline has begun to diminish. It's like a skier slowing down when they reach the flat zone in the middle of the slope. The possibility of a breakout is imminent however, that's where my analogy breaks down because share prices do not get chairlifts.

When I began working on TA, I realized that these indicators to be the most difficult to wrap my mind around, even though my experience was filled with stats and data manipulation. They weren't so intuitive as say candlesticks or price charts. If you're having difficult time with any of them, you're certainly not alone.

Stochastic

The term "stochastic," if you search for it in the dictionary doesn't necessarily mean that this is a reliable indicator. "Stochastic" refers to "having an unpredictable probability distribution that could be analysed statistically, but isn't forecasted precisely." Furthermore being interested in forecasts which is why how valuable will a stochastic indicator prove to prove?

But, the stochastic can be a useful indicator of the speed of stocks. The person who invented it, George Lane, actually thought of it as if it is a rocket that is likely to descend to the earth and then crash then it must slow down near the highest point of the parabola. Spacecrafts only stop when they are moving too fast.

It does this by analyzing the price variation over the time frame (typically five days). It examines the closing price every day with the absolute highest and the absolute low of five days. If it's at an extremely high level indicates that prices are closing near the top of the spectrum A very low value suggests an extreme downside momentum.

The stochastic doesn't display "oversold" and "overbought," though; it only shows the rate of price increase. To illustrate think about driving around 120 miles per hour in your vehicle that's a high speed, however it does not mean that you'll be immediately forced in a downward direction. Instead, you may continue to go for quite a long time.

It's a great confirmation of breakout signals derived that are derived from the chart of prices. If the stochastic continues to move upwards with a rapid pace, it is a sign that the trend will persist, which is why if you took an indication of price for an outbreak and the price has moved up, it is best to continue to trade and possibly scale back and increase your stop-loss levels to reflect the price of entry.

Another type of signal is when the price is moving up and down and then the stochastic begins to move downwards. Even if it's an insignificant divergence, and the stochastic line only a tiny bit sagging and you are able to see a slight dip, you may want to search for a reversal. The stochastic tells the market that it is slowing even though that could be a sign that the price increase is less steep If the stock has seen a significant amount of buyers' interest and has increased very quickly and the stochastic is telling you that things are likely to become rough. If there's no buy-in left, the price could be able to fall quickly.

The same signal can be used in reverse in the event that prices have been moving down, but now you can see the stochastic lifting up. Reversal might be in the near future. This is likely to be the only moment when the stochastic signals an accurate signal instead of simply confirmation.

This chart displays the complete stochastic, with the highest at the top. "Realty Income" is among the most highly regarded US real estate companies and offers huge dividends. See how big the stochastic fluctuations. It is interesting to note that the biggest shifts into negative territory usually precede a downturn and the major swings upwards occur prior to an upward trend. (Of course, it's important to keep in mind that the massive decline in March of 2020 was triggered by an event; it was the first sign of the Covid-19 epidemic in the west. I don't think that the stochastic can really be predicting this! However, if you'd noticed that you were little more wealthy, at least.)

Relative Strength Index (RSI)

The index is a measure of the proportion of upwards to downwards price movements. It does not consider how significant the change was, but rather how much the stock went either way or up in the course of the day. Thus, for example 10 days of RSI begins by looking at the number of days did the stock rise? 7. And then down? 3. (If the stock is closed at a certain at the same level throughout the day and it is zero for the day.) The figures are then averaged, which means we have +7/10 and the minus is 3/10. (That's an easy method to accomplish it. Some people also employ EMA and more sophisticated statistical smoothing techniques, which will only make you confused, so let's remove that.)

The only thing we have to do is figure out how much of the upward and downward moves, called RS and then calculate we can calculate the "RSI is 100 times (100 * (1 + RS))."

If you've read that, then you've likely guessed that the index ranges from zero to 100. If you're not following the RSI, that's no problem. It's a good idea regardless that it's the RSI is a gauge of how frequently the price is increasing versus the amount of time it's been falling. Most stocks be trading between 30 to 70 according to the RSI and this indicates an acceptable balance between the buyers and sellers. However, an RSI over 70 indicates that the stock may be overvalued--it could be about to drop, whereas if the RSI is lower than 30, the stock may be overvalued, and its price could be set to climb. (Some traders prefer an 80-20 range to make their trades, giving the trader fewer, but better signals.)

In the graph above you can see when the RSI falls below 30 lines for the first time, it makes a small rally however, the next time it's real. Too many buyers have been in the second phase of the downtrend. Also, when there's a breakout the price really accelerates. After that, when the RSI is close to 70, there's a slight dip, but it's until it crosses the 70 line that the price truly plummets. In the meantime, far enough buyers have invested--some have bought too many shares--and at the time the decline in price begins the buyers "catch the cold" and then sell. It is interesting to think of the RSI line just crossing above the central lines (the straight line that is the light blue). Is it likely to stay at the same mark? Could it be headed towards oversold territory?

What exactly do we mean by "overbought" or "oversold"? When a stock is priced too high the stock may have seen many articles written regarding it in the news. Numerous investors have bought. The price has continued to move upwards, but at present everybody who is interested in the stock is getting. There aren't any new investors to boost the price and some of the buyers who bought early may be looking to earn a profit, which could cause the price to fall. The stock is "oversold," the stock has seen numerous sellers would like to leave, possibly due to poor performance in earnings or a reduction in dividends and the majority of those who were looking to sell has done so. If a few buyers who aren't conventional come into the market believing that the stock is cheap and it is a bargain, it may rise.

RSI is particularly adept in spotting an end to a lengthy decline or the top of a spike. This is where the price chart may not be providing any information that is useful. If you're trying to be able to enter at an end of correction, look at the RSI!

The majority of traders utilize fourteen-day RSI. Based on the timeframes you would like to trade, you could choose nine (for trading on a day basis) and 30 (for intermediate-term traders).

There are many methods to utilize RSI. It is the first method that provides a great sense of the trends. If the RSI is able to break it's trend line it could be the first clue that a reversal is imminent prior to seeing it on an analysis of the chart price.

Second, you should search at RSI divergence. Find out when the RSI is in opposition from the price line. If a price has an upper high, search at the previous highest point, then draw a line between to the previous high and. Then, take a look at the RSI below on your chart of price, and look for the latest level, which might not be directly underneath the price's highest and draw the line that connects it to the prior highest high. Take a take a look at the direction of these two lines. If they're moving to the same place, then that's excellent. It's how you'd expect the price to be: it's rising and the share is closing the majority of days higher than it is down. However, If you notice that the RSI line is moving downwards , not upwards as the price of shares, it's an indication of a negative signal; you have what's called "bearish divergence" that's a great "sell indication."

Technical Volume Indicators

Alongside price action, the second principal element of analysis is the volume. It's a simple idea, at first however it is frequently not fully understood to its maximum extent. This lack of understanding could mostly be explained by the somewhat higher-level abstraction of the concept as compared to the fundamental directional premise of price actions. But, don't worry as there will be an array of distinctive diagrams that will enhance the understanding you have of volumes. Also, regardless of whether you're new to the field or an experienced investor or trader and trader, you can further enhance your knowledge about volume.

In the beginning, prior to beginning the diagrams, it's important to remember that it is traditionally simpler to study the volume of markets that are able to effectively and accurately report the volume. This means that the stock as well as cryptocurrency market are the most appropriate. For example, Forex markets. Commodity Bonds and other market types aren't as secure for continuous disclosure of trading volume accessible to the general public. In many instances, these markets do not display volumes at all in the majority of charting platforms.

Cryptocurrencies and stocks can be easily measured in terms of amount of shares purchased and sold on the stock market, as well as the amount of each cryptocurrency that is traded. Other markets are generally more difficult to monitor in terms of quantity. For instance the Forex market is likely to have difficulties tracking the currencies that are exchanged across the world, particularly when it comes to reporting cash transactions seamlessly, as well as exchange currencies in less-connected and transparent areas of the world.

Stock markets, in contrast, operates with fixed times and operates for specific geographic regions. Every shares sold and bought is tracked easily and easily. The same is true for cryptocurrency although the market is not as rigid in terms of working hours and does not have a fixed geographic region. The digital ledger that is built into blockchain technologies is just as simple, if not easier--to change the volume of trades.

In this regard that said, it's not fair to say that cryptocurrency and stocks are better than other options in terms of analysis. We will be able to see this in other examples which don't show trading volume charts can be analysed to great advantage using price action alone.

It's a simple concept It's a simple concept, right?

If a specific trading session, say an entire day on a daily chart result in an increase in price and, in this case it is normal to see the bar for volume being displayed in green on almost all platforms. As an example, in the chart above this could be an investment that has was up in price today, and the amount in shares exchanged was five million. Also, it could be a different chart with the price falling and 2 million shares traded as well one which increased in value and included 1.8 million traded shares.

In order to take the idea further, let's look at market volume and markets. The following representations in graphs of these will give an easy explanation that allows one to grasp the significance of volume visually within many different charting situations, all without the need to utilize indicators. There are a lot of indicators with the intention of improving or aid in comprehend the meaning of price action and volume. However, the reality is that they're complementary and not essential. It is possible to achieve amazing analysis and results from investing and trading without the use of an indicator of any type.

Then, as you might already know the sun is full of energy. Sometimes this energy may be concentrated into sunspots. Be assured that this will not turn into an astronomy course but it's an extremely useful analogy.

Each sunspot is the number of shares in the stock. The diagram is comprised of 13 spots. To make things clear each spot is the equivalent of 1 million shares the imaginary stock. That's a total of that there exist 13 million shares in existence. Additionally the middle of the circle is a symbol for those shares "outstanding," or, that is to say they're shares that aren't held by the company who issued the stock, instead, but rather shares are being sold and are traded on the market.

The points in the triangles are the shares the company owns or positions held by investors and traders. That is, the 8 million shares that are in the triangles are made up of shares held by the company which issued the stock or they're shares purchased and in the hands of investors and traders on the market.

In the market for cryptocurrency this could appear similar to the circles that represents the currency that has been mined , and the triangles that represent the currency that is yet to be mined, or currency that is owned by investors and traders.

The same concept of this diagram could be used to apply to other markets, such as Forex as well as commodity derivatives. The circle is the thing that is available on the market, it symbolizes offering to buy and sell that are ready to be exchanged between the market players (traders or investors). The triangles are also the triangles represent the amount of securities that are not available to be purchased or sold.

Similar to the energy of the sun, stocks or any other security, for that matter move continuously. Stocks are always traded and bought which is the reason prices fluctuate. You've probably heard this, too. However, what's more difficult for the majority of people to grasp is the relationship between volume and the size of price movements. It is simple to comprehend that a significant amount of selling can lower the price substantially if more shares were sold than purchased at the moment. This could be evident through the display of a large red bar.

But, what can be more difficult and sometimes frustrating to figure out is the reason why the prices on charts may fluctuate significantly, even when volume seems to be at a low.

In the following diagram, we will have 1 million shares being purchased (hence the dot in green) and no shares sold. It is obvious that such a scenario is almost impossible to imagine however, this diagram serves to better understand the volume. So, there's an excess of buying into markets for the company. One million more shares bought instead of sold is significant enough to propel the price up. As with the general rule of thumb that is 45 degrees for increases prices, there's no number or percentage of how much buying/selling quantity is available before it results in a specific amount as a percentage of price fluctuation.

But, prices increase naturally in the event of a significant disparity between buyers and sellers, as in this case. Similar is the case in the opposite case of a substantial amount of selling versus buying, which results in the price dropping. Every chart will differ dependent on the kind of chart, the market, and the conditions. Additionally, a principle to remember is the fact that, as "liquid" the stock is, the more imbalance of sellers and buyers is required to push the price substantially. A chart that has a high volume is considered to be liquid, whereas one that has low volume isn't. It is logical since moving prices of liquid stock of a huge firm would require an extremely large volumes in comparison to the less volume required to move the price of the stock of a smaller business.

The trade-off is that a smaller stock with less volume will have a larger bid-ask spread as there are less buyers and sellers to reach an agreement on prices for trading. Conversely stocks that are highly liquid will have a smaller bid-ask spread since there are many buyers who can provide more choice in the selling and buying price.

The greater the gap between buyers and sellers the more dramatic the price change. In this particular instance, there 2 million shares purchased and sold, which increases the severity of the price increase.

In addition, there is a very extreme example below, which has an even greater gap between sellers and buyers. This results in a near-vertical rise. A similar scenario could be triggered, for example, when the market reacts positively to an earnings report.

In the present, after the additional 1 million shares sold the inequity or the gap of selling more shares than buying remains. But, the current price increase is less since the gap has been reduced to 2 million shares purchased rather than sold. Additionally there are only 1 million shares are ready to trade on the market right now. 8 million shares remain being held by investors and traders or are owned by the company that owns the stock. In any event 8 million shares are in the possibility of being traded in the future.

Then, another 3 million shares are added to the market. It doesn't matter if they are shares owned by the company or purchased by investors or traders. The result is that 3 million shares are being added to the market.

Today, a million shares have been soldand, in the end it leads to net reduction in value of the stock, but it is not yet at its peak during this particular session of trading.

But, the current upward trend is much less, and this can be seen in the way that the price rise has returned to what it was in the past when just 1 million shares were purchased instead of sold. The requirement to buy 3 million shares buy side as compared to the two million shares sold on the sell-side still an impressive amount, however it isn't the same as it was.

In the end, the price is almost unchanged and is essentially level since 3 million shares are present on both the buy - and sell-side. In real-time markets, this could never occur however, in the interest of demonstrating it is assumed that the figures on both sides are the same. In actuality, the volume of buying and selling will be similar, however, they would not be exactly the same when trading sessions produce little or no price change.

The moment is now the time to begin an idea of what occurs when the market reverses (in this instance towards the downside) in the event that more sales are introduced to the market.

Buyers who purchased prior to the time of trading start to sell. The market's scales are tilted to the left as greater selling pressures are brought in the markets.

This is the opposite to what was seen in the past, and the above chart illustrates the shift in the balance of the market after a sharp shift to an accelerated decline.

The diagram above illustrates the return of balance to an increase in value due to a shift to more selling than buying on the market throughout the session of trade. The rapid shifts shown in the two previous diagrams, are common during times of uncertainty or decline, like during recessions. But, these features can also be seen in charts that are volatile like biotech stocks or highly speculative times for commodities and currencies.

Like the numerous synonyms that are used to describe the basic notions of up, down and sideways movements to describe the basic elements of price action, the volume is also a subject of plenty of similar terminologies. The volume is often described as, and is frequently referred to as the force, energy or pressure, as well as intent, interest and consensus of the market. It determines the size of price movement to a significant extent. In subsequent chart examples, we will find many examples of how certain patterns of volume are in sync with specific events in price movement.

Divergences

What is a correlation divergence?

The answer is straightforward It is evident in its name! It's a reversal of closely related assets. For instance, when two assets with a similarity to each other or, in another sense "move in a similar direction," fall out of the correlation. A particular asset may shift in a different direction from its counterpart. This can be seen often in indices such as the "Standard and Poor's 500 Index," the "Dow Jones Industrial Average," and the "NASDAQ." It is difficult to see if you are not looking for this type of movement, so a trader needs to actively search for these particular criteria to get logical use from the formation--hopefully. A different term for this kind of analysis is "relative Strength Analysis."

In addition, the American indexes have a correlation however, many other investments interact. For instance EUR/USD and GBP/USD commonly referred to in the context of "Fiber and Cable." While the correlation between these two majors might have less strength than the other however, it's still important to note. The AUD/USD pair as well as the NZD/USD pair, referred to by the name of "Aussie as well as Kiwi," tend to be strongly in sync with one another in the majority of cases. Additionally the silver and gold are frequently parallelized.

Certain stocks could be compared with their respective sector. For example, ($AMZN) and NASDAQ (as as of August 2020). The goal is to evaluate the two to determine which is more successful or less than the other. This analysis will give you an insights into what asset is stronger or weak. It will help in determining the areas where high-risk trades could occur. The ideal trader will search for opportunities to buy assets that are more profitable than their counterparts. This is because you are purchasing something that could be considered to be solid and you are avoiding weaker assets, which is considered slow-moving assets. The outperformer is referred to as an exemplary leader. If a shorting scenario is in play the laggard is the ideal candidate to short due to the weakness.

Image 1 of Correlation Divergence

Let's look at what I'm talking about. If we look at an a line chart or candlestick chart, then it might be beneficial to cross-check the two assets that you've decided to match against each other. We will need to decide whether the buy and outperformer are or the underperformer and the short in the context of whatever market condition that we are currently in. Below depicts the type of chart we'll be studying in future charts.

In this illustration it is evident that the top asset creating a low that is lower, while that on the lower side is making the higher low. Whichever asset you choose to use for the bottom it is the top performer. It is the asset you must be looking for a higher price. It's particularly beneficial when it happens in a very short timeframe and the price is at a higher level of support. This could be a sign of a shift into the markets. The retracements that follow could be beneficial to traders who is looking to increase the price of this asset.

Correlation Divergence Image 2

See how EUR/USD reached an upper low, while GBP/USD made an lower low? This is your correlation divergence. No indicators are required, just basic charting. Based on my knowledge, this implies that the presence of more cash (and when I say more money, I'm talking about intelligent money) is in favor of the higher price of EUR/USD. Are you noticing any other thing? Perhaps an institution candle is in someplace? It's pretty cool, isn't it? It's all beginning to connect.

Correlation Divergence Image 3

Let's take a examine the shorting scenario above. It is evident that EUR/USD in this particular instance is not performing as well as GBP/USD. This is an indication of weakening. The market continues to decline with lower prices, and potential profits to those who have shorted market.

What is the reason why the correlation Divergence Relevant?

As of now, you've seen some pivotal events in the market. The significance of the divergences in these instances is they possibly create tops and bottoms in the market. There is a chance that you will not be able to spot the exact high or low however knowing when a trend shift is likely to occur can be useful for traders. I've seen these happen in all timespans.

The method I use to determine divergence for my own trading might be a tool that you could find helpful in your own study of the market. I hope you be able to use it since it is among my top tools. At the moment I'm sure that a lot of you would like additional examples, so I've included additional examples. Enjoy!

Correlation Divergence Image 4

Images 5 of Correlation Divergence

Images 6 of Correlation Divergence

In relation to the stock market collapse of 2020, many affirm that you can't predict your market... Would you think you agree?

Correlation Divergence Image 7

Correlation Divergence Image 8

Correlation Divergence Image 9

The Correlation Divergence image 10

Correlation Divergence Image 11

Correlation Divergence Image 12

Correlation Divergence Image 13

Correlation Divergence Image 14

Are you aware of the difference between the first charts and the more recent ones? Do you see that I began adding some of the concepts in this book to the charts... It's cool you think? I'm sure that you have noticed that I put lots of examples of opportunities to buy instead of selling opportunities. This is because stocks tend to be generally positive. But, there are also shorting or selling opportunities that operate in the same exactly opposite. I have left two charts of selling for you to refer to However, it's going to be your responsibility to build yourself and learn for yourself. You didn't think I'd give you everything to you, did you?

Chapter 12: Errors In Technical Analysis

This is a collection of errors in technical analysis that you must take note of. Many struggle with this field and consider it risky, but should you stay clear of the traps that are listed below, your odds will be significantly increased. These are the most common errors that can be made in the field of technical analysis.

Trading to achieve the purpose of achieving a Specific Price Goal

It's not a problem in the long run, so long you are able to keep it simple. It is possible to define your goals as the most and least you'd like for your trading to transform in the coming days. This is easy since you know what you're trying to achieve and the place where the trade should conclude.

Trading on the Specific Time Frame

It is possible to define very brief-term goals, medium-term targets and long-term goals; however it's not recommended to define each interval between these in order to avoid leading into confusion as well as an overwhelmed brain (rumination).

Following the Crowd

If you are planning to invest in the market, you must be aware that every choice you make isn't your own decision. You'll be trading alongside thousands of other traders. A lot of them will consider your choice to be an element of the market (known in the industry as "herding") and that is the way markets change, especially at the beginning. The thing that determines the direction of markets is greed and fear.

Leverage

Trading with leverage means that if your investment goes against you by more than 10 your position is closed , and you could lose more than the cash capital. It can happen quickly and without warning. This is not the kind of thing you'd prefer to see. If you're trading using leverage, please make sure the accuracy of your verified price for stop-loss entered in the present.

Panic Selling

Don't sell when the price is in decline, sell only when the market has risen and you're sure the market will move higher. Many traders sell when the stock is at their lowest however, they aren't aware of how quickly these changes are likely to reverse. You can lower your risk by focusing on support zones (at the upper or lower line) and buying the stock once the stock breaks through these support zones (breakouts happen rapidly).

Tight Stops

If you're trading on longer time frames (5 minutes to 1 hour) and you are trading on the higher time frames, then you cannot afford to lose your position. Because these movements could drain you of cash and result in you having no funds to fund the next trade. The term "tight stop" refers to a stop that will leave you with only a small profit (or the possibility of losing) once your position is close.

The No-Touch Rule

If you wish to succeed in your technical analysis, you should not make any moves unless you are certain you can be sure that your market is going to remain in the direction it was following the trail of bands/support zones, etc. If you're not certain then, you could set your stops trailing at exactly the same distance from the market, however this time you should use an instance of price movement (e.g. or the candlestick pattern).

Breakouts

Breakouts occur very fast, however when you're not sure it will move in this direction, you could move your stops a bit ahead of it, as long as it remains within its support/resistance area/line. The price at which the breakout occurs is the time when the majority of traders begin to cut losses off the table since they believe they've successfully achieved their goal. This is exactly what you want to avoid. You must keep an eye on the markets and avoid getting afraid of trading once the breakout has occurred.

Fakeouts

This is why many traders are caught when they examine the "fake off candle" This is because they think that there's another fakeout coming up and that it will go on the same path (well they think this because it's the way it's always been to their advantage). But this time, it could be different. It is important to ensure that you remain within the limit of your stop-loss and also trail your stops to the market to avoid fakeouts.

Breakdowns

It's a common occurrence and the mistake is caused by traders who fear an apparent breakdown. Sometimes, this happens for just only a few candle but this doesn't necessarily mean that the market is going to move in that direction for the duration of your trading. Set your stops ahead of any possible breakdown, and wait for a Reversal candle to develop before making any decisions on what to do next.

Odds and Averages

When you trade, you have to think differently about the profitability. This is the result of ordered or linear thinking. The market, however is chaotic and linear thinking will take you nowhere.

Instead, you should consider the odds and averages. Averages suggest that you have be concerned about the size of your average loss as well as your average win size. Try to reduce the former while increasing the latter. Be aware that when we speak of averages, we're not always discussing reducing the total amount of losses. The average can be reduced in two ways: either by reducing the amount of your losses, or increasing the amount of trades that lose but keeping the total of your losses the same. This is a change in your thinking that you have to make.

This way of thinking will help you think about chances because in chaotic systems, the only thing you can bet on are chances that will play out in the long term. For instance, if play a game of chance, can you know beforehand what the outcome will either be heads or tails? It's probably not. If someone asked you to estimate the ratio of heads versus tails in 10,000 flips, then you could fairly predict that there will consist of 5000 head and 5000 tails. It's possible that you're off by a couple of flips in either direction but you'll probably be close in percentage.

In actual fact, the more the number of turns that you make, the lower your chance of error. This is due to the probabilities inherent in a pattern which occurs in a chaotic environment manifest themselves in the long term. Your trading strategy follows precisely an example of a pattern. The market is a chaotic and unstable system. So, you should concentrate on the way you execute your plan as it should be carried out repeatedly, and only worry about the profitability over the long-term.

Contrast this with the typical approach of traders that seek to be the best at every trade. This isn't possible because no strategy or pattern can be proven to be correct all the time. If we were talking about directions, I'd probably spend longer on this issue, but the truth is that options handle the ambiguity by themselves.

This is due to the fact that you don't need to be concerned about trading options. You simply enter and monitor the trade. It's good to have a directionality, but even in the event that you're wrong your losses will be very limited and you're more likely beat losers than winners.

However, you must always be thinking of your plan in terms of the odds. There are two primary measures to gauge this. First is the winning rate of your system. It is the percentage of winners that you have. The second one is your payout ratio which is the size of your average win divided by the size of your loss average.

Both measures will decide how effective your method is. Both are linked to one another and a rise in one is typically matched with a decrease in the other. It requires a highly skilled trader to boost both simultaneously.

Risk per Trade

The quantitative aspect of risk management in relation to options trading is much less than the risks you have to be aware of when trading in a more direct manner. However, that does not mean you don't have anything to be concerned about. The most important metric of all is the trading risk. Risk per trade determines your overall profitability.

How much risk should you take per trade? The general consensus is that you should limit the risk to 2percent of your capital. If you are using options for trading it's appropriate. Actually, when you've mastered your skills and are able to spot opportunities more clearly I'd suggest boosting the level to a higher.

One thing you need to be aware of is that you need to make sure that your risk per trade stays level constant for it to have any impact. It is possible to see a beautiful set-up and believe that there is no chance of being unsuccessful, but the reality is that you're not sure what will happen. Even the most attractive setup is at risk of being unsuccessful, while the most ugly arrangement you can think of could yield making you money, so do not change the size of your positions according to how it looks.

How to calculate the size of your positions to trade is fairly simple. Each strategy has an amount that is fixed for maximum risk. The capital risk is divided by the amount which will give you the size of your position. Round it down to the closest total number, since you are only able to purchase whole lot sizes in size of contracts.

Let's take an example. For instance, suppose you have a maximum risk of $50 per lot in the transaction. The capital you have is 10,000. The risk for each trade is at 2%. The amount of risk you're taking on the trade is the equivalent of 2% of 10,000 which is 200. Divide this number by 50 and you'll have four. Thus, your total position is four contracts, or 400 shares. (You'll purchase the contracts and however, not shares.)

What is the reason to ensure that your risk per trade is constant? Remember that your win and loss size is vital in the calculation of your profit. Together with the success rate of your strategy determine how much profit you'll earn. If you constantly change the amount of risk you take on each trade, you'll change the sizes of your losses and wins. It's possible to argue that because this is an average you could adjust the amounts to represent the average.

My answer to this is: how do you determine which trades you should adjust prior to? You don't know which will result in winning or losing and therefore you don't be able to determine which sizes of trades to adjust to match the standard. Therefore, ensure that you are the same across all trades, while letting the mathematics do the work for you.

In addition to the risk for each trade other basic metrics that you need to be tracking in your risk management strategy for quantitative risk.

Chapter 13: The Financial Statements As Well

As The Fundamental Analysis

Fundamental Analysis Fundamental Analysis is based on one of the primary tools utilized in the economic system, and that's accounting statements. The objective in this paper is to demonstrate to the various stakeholders, both internal as well as external, the economic and fiscal performance of the business. It is a form of assurance that the company provides to each potential customer or investor. In addition, this document permits the business that prepared it to run its business in a proper manner. It is, however, an obligation of law that listed businesses produce and release their financial statements that should be accessible to each investor or other interested party. Additionally, the openness of international markets for companies has forced the law to to standardize the information documents in order to make it easier to compare with the accounts of various businesses or between accounting statements for the identical company over different time frames. Of obviously, a comparison of this sort can only be conducted between companies that are in the same industry.

In actuality the majority of fundamental analysts are unable to conduct an analysis that is based on the balance sheet because they do not usually have the required skills to interpret the indices in an appropriate manner, and thus misinterpreting the performance of the company. Sometimes the balance sheet may be written in a complicated manner, which may be confusing to potential investors.

To better understand quickly the overall health of an economic system it is beneficial to concentrate on three of the documents of financial statements, specifically the Balance Sheet and the Income Statement, as well as the ratios of financial statements.

2.1 Budget structure

It is the balance sheet and income statement that are principal elements of the financial statements. They are often accompanied in order for explanation, and incorporated with the explanation note as well as The Cash Flow Statement.

The Balance Sheet provides a layout with two distinct sections. In the first section of the document, which is on from the left side of the prospectus are the assets; to the right will be the obligations. The two sections should be in line to produce an accurate Balance Sheet.

Its income report, on other hand, is in an scalar format, which is divided into four parts. When we begin the creation of the Income Statement the fundamental components are identified in order to analyze the financial statements with the help of indicators.

The Balance Sheet as well as the Income Statement have to be classified in order to show additional elements that in the earlier draft were not visible.

2.1.1 - - Balance Sheet

The Balance Sheet is the place to group all of the passive and active components of a business. The active elements are fixed assets, investments regardless of whether they are tangible, intangible, or current assets that are financial in nature, comprised of receivables, inventories and cash. In the case of passive elements in contrast are the equity of shareholders and the provision for risk as well as charges. They also include the segregation payments as well as the outstanding debts. Alongside these components accruals and deferrals should be divided equally between both liabilities and assets, based on the financial situation.

Net assets are an outcome of the differences between passive and active elements. This way the individual interested in the matter will be able to determine the true value of the business is when all the loans listed on the accounts are paid. Thus net assets are the amount of equity that the business has to complete the production phase and, in addition, how much are the sources of external financing held by the business. Naturally, a healthy business is one that relies solely on the capital in its possession, and not having to rely on loans or other financing that is provided by credit institutions.

The final goal for the balance sheet in Financial Statements is show the capital structure and the financial position of a specific company. This is the reason that balance sheets are seen to be one of the primary documents that has to be scrutinized by analysts of fundamental importance.

2.1.2 Income Statement

The Income Statement is comprised of all items related to revenues and costs that occurred during the specified time frame that generally falls within the calendar year. Through the study of the profit and loss Account it can be determined whether the business has earned profits during the fiscal year, which is to say whether it is a profitable company, or has suffered losses. In some cases it is possible that the business closes its budget using a draw which is a the perfect balance of costs and revenue.

The process of determining how much profits or losses a business is quite easy. It is essential to calculate the cost of revenues and profits mathematically. If a positive number is achieved, that is that the revenue exceeds the expenses that is, there will be profit. On the other hand If the revenues are less than the cost the loss will occur.

The Income Statement contains a wealth of other fascinating information for investors who are considering investing. For starters, it is possible to analyze the results of the business based on the product or production area. It is possible to figure out which product is as the flagship product of the company, latest products that are launched on the market , and the areas of weakness of the business. In addition, by using income statements, it's possible to evaluate the company's assets and compare them to the earnings earned.

Another element that is related to the Income Statement is its ability to show everyone interested in the matter the level of the work done by each manager, in relation to the duties carried out. Management aspects of an organization are among the most significant and yet the least understood aspects of an asset. In reality, the success of an organization is contingent on the concepts and strategies employed by these departments. The strategies must be able to deal with suppliers, customers and, most importantly, competitors and guide the company to maximize profit. But the aim is not always reached.

The primary difference between the balance sheet and income statement is the latter provides the static view of the assets of a business in the form of assets, which are in place at the time that the financial statements are compiled and are therefore accounted for at the close of the year. In contrast, it analyzes and depicts the changing economic

148

environment throughout the year, namely that of the revenue stream.

2.1.3 Notes to the accounts of cash flows and financial statements

While less crucial for the accomplishment of the goals that are set by an analyst fundamental however, the financial statements include two other documents, which are they are the Notes to the Financial Statements and the Financial Statement.

The notes for the financial Statements explain to all people involved in the implementation of the financial statements, and the foundational principles used within them are. They also serve the purpose of explaining the specific items in a concise and timely way. This document also is a key element in the regularization of accounting statements. In reality, the foundations upon the basis of which budgets are drawn out are diverse and utilize totally different methods and logic according to their perception regarding the marketplace and economy. Therefore, it is important to clarify what strategies the management has used for the execution of the budget and how each line item should be understood by the concerned individuals.

Financial Statement Financial Statement, on the contrary is a report that was introduced in Italy was made mandatory in 2015. However, it is a crucial element for the analysis of financial statements. Its purpose is to define those assets that are liquid, by breaking them down and looking at the liquid assets in that it provides clarity and clarity of the value as well as their development, depending on the value at the beginning and the end each year is listed. Furthermore Financial Statements provide a comprehensive overview of the Financial Statement analyzes the financial flows that are derived from individual sector of the company, in particular from those pertaining to the operating activities as well as from the investment sector as well as from the finance sectors. The significance of this report is to provide the basic analyst with a continuous analysis of the corporate earnings.

The stock of assets, which is static doesn't allow us to analyze the trends as well as the performance of the firm in the marketplace, and thus provides only an overview of the overall the health of the organization. Thus, it is essential to go deeper into the flows and study them in depth so that we can determine what the true business trend might be.

Additionally that, the preparation of accounts is built upon the implementation of certain rules set out in national law or international regulations. The most significant are those that pertain to prudential practices, which mean that only positive elements are required to be included on the balance sheet however, negative components can be assumed to be present; to economic competence that implies that only the expenses and revenue relating to the fiscal year have to be reported regardless of the date when they are due to have financial implications; the predominance of the material over the form, in which it is imperative to evaluate the economic value of particular items.

2.2 Analyzing the financial statement indicators that are useful in Fundamental Analysis

The process of budgeting is a highly complex procedure that requires technical expertise as well as a deep understanding of the area. The goal is to collect data that is otherwise not recognized, specifically, it focuses on information regarding managing the business. The analysis concentrates on things that appear on the Balance Sheet and the Income Statement for the final year of the fiscal year. It gives important indicators, which are valuable to the basic analyst and reveal the real condition of the business. In order to be able to utilize these however, it is essential to revise and change the classification of the financial statements in accordance with different methods, based on the purpose of the analysis and the factors we plan to examine.

2.2.1 - Earnings Before Taxes, Interest, Amortization and Depreciation

The primary measure of the financial statements is the Earnings before Taxes, Interest, Depreciation and Amortization, more commonly referred to by the abbreviation EBITDA. Its purpose is to give the analyst a clear assessment of the wealth generated by the firm, and just in its specific industry, which is the primary one. It is also referred to by the name Gross Operating Margin or more simply MOL. In actuality it is a measure that exploits the income statement's reclassification by adjusting it to the Added Value requirement to produce an intermediate outcome that is purely operational in nature without tax, interest amortization, depreciation and taxes remaining covered.

A benefit of the calculation of EBITDA is the ability to easily compare your Gross Operating Margin (GOM) of the financial statement to that included in different financial reports, allowing you to have an immediate picture of the business that has the most efficient operating performance. Actually the process of standardizing EBITDA has been implemented in the past to make it easier for investors, as well as fundamental analysts who calculate their earnings based on studying the characteristics of the company.

2.2.2 Return On Equity

The Return on Equity indicator, also known as ROE is among the ratios of return on equity. This indicator can be used to evaluate the financial performance of a business in percentage terms, because it compares Net Income with Net Capital. This determines how much of an investment has resulted in revenue. To be able to get a true picture of the financial performance of the company however, it's important to assess the amount of ROE calculated with other indicators of investment to be able to determine the opportunity cost associated with the initial investment made by the business. The variation that is derived from this analysis is referred to within the realm of economics as a risk cost. If the risk premium is based on a value of zero, it is a sign that it is not worth to invest in that business because the investor will get the same outcome by not investing at all.

2.2.3 Return On Investment

The indicator for Return On Investment is also known by The ROI acronym, is designed to demonstrate the efficiency of a specific company that is based on the management aspect. The ROI does not take into account the sources utilized to generate the revenue throughout the course of. This indicator is utilized for fundamental analyses to determine the ROI on invested capital is.

To meet its purpose To achieve its goal, to meet its objective, ROI measures the total operating results of the business with the average of capital that was invested in the same time.

However, the basic analyst must be aware of the shortcomings with this indicator. For one, the ROI grows as you progress through the financial year as the balance sheet will be the most affected by the rise in depreciation's value. A third negative aspect about ROI is the fact that it is a relation between to a stock's value, which is, the capital invested to a flow, which is the operating earnings generated.

Chapter 14: The Fundamental Analysis On

The Stock Market And Forex

Fundamental Analysis and the Technical Analysis Fundamental Analysis and the Technical Analysis provide the best methods to evaluate the changes in the financial markets, and particularly, of that of the Forex market. Without these two methods traders would not have a solid foundation on to base their forecasts and investment could turn out to be bankruptcy. The traders rely in particular on Fundamental Analysis to try to determine what the direction of a certain trend might be over the long term. Naturally it is Fundamental Analysis is a must. Fundamental Analysis carried out on the financial markets will pay on the prices of securities, financial instruments and currencies in the market in which the trader plans to invest. It is logical however that an analysis like this should be conducted by a skilled trader or by genuine analysts who conduct these analyses as a profession. It is because novice investors aren't equipped with the abilities to properly describe economic developments that could impact the financial markets.

The general approach to Fundamental Analysis applied on the financial markets concentrates on macroeconomic reasons, which means that it focuses on the factors that alter the demand curve and offer even in the biggest financial market on the planet that is, the Forex. The fundamental analyst focuses his or her focus on the development of countries however, they also look towards the possibility of a common trend that will unite a set of states with the same geographical, ethnic, or cultural characteristics as well as the overall global economic growth. But, what really affects the financial market is the decisions made by the both international and national political officials. They directly influence the economic performance of states as the connection between the realm of politics and finance is immediate. Additional factors that impact basic analysis are the impact of the social as well as the impact of the climate on trade and the cost of items. These are elements which should not be ignored that can assist traders understand ahead of time the potential market fluctuations, thereby generating greater profits.

3.1 The stock market: analysis of the sector and valuation of companies

One of the main goals of fundamental analysts is to discover the value the shares is so that they can compare it to the value that is portrayed in the market. So the investor has the possibility of investing in securities that are undervalued, believing that they'll soon realize their actual value, due to the standard market corrections. The Fundamental Analytic approach to the stock market is based upon the steps each investor has to put into practice.

The first stage is the study of all macroeconomic factors that could affect the market. In the beginning, the analysis should be divided by geographic area and economic region. So traders can choose for markets that are considered to be more favorable, based on the outcomes that are derived from this analysis.

The third phase involves an analysis of the sector. This is a complex analysis that considers all businesses that are on the market, in which it is investing and considers all possible future scenarios. The analysis of the sector goes beyond the realm of only finance and economy, since it includes the realm of IT, social, and cultural issues. Naturally, in order to perform an analysis like this you need certain skills and an in-depth knowledge of the market.

The final and third phase is the assessment of firms that are for sale. The trader must analyze the financial statements released by every company, and must classify the Balance Sheet as well as the Income Statement, and on these financial statements, apply the ratios of financial statements. This way investors can see what the actual value of the business is. The value is then measured against the value the company puts out in the marketplace, and in the event of a difference that is derived in it. As a result, the investor is able to invest with the highest probability of a successful outcome.

3.2 the intrinsic worth of equity

A single of the crucial aspects of Fundamental Analysis is for a trader to comprehend the meaning behind what is the true value an asset. The concept of intrinsic value has an extremely simple concept to comprehend from a conceptual perspective, however in actual practice, it may be a difficult thing to determine.

But, it is essential to begin with the assumption that the true value of an investment instrument or asset is an abstract value. This value is possible in real life only if investors were rational people that do not make mistakes and operate using ideal benchmarks. Only by doing this, actually, can the real value of an investment product or market be realized.

Finding this value is feasible, at the very least and is over all, extremely beneficial. To accomplish this an analyst with a solid understanding should examine a company across all areas including the management, the strategies employed and from the investment that are made, to financial reports taking into consideration how financial resources come from and their capacity to transform into earnings. Once an analyst is aware of what the value of a particular economic reality could be, he or must analyze the value it is taking in the market. Based on that, he or must make an investment of his own. The fundamental idea upon which to base your trading but the reality is that in the long run the value the financial asset along with its actual value generally match. If the value portrayed from the markets by the company is less than its intrinsic value and the analyst is not satisfied, then he is likely to invest in the stock being aware that, in the end, the two will coincide.

So, it's feasible to say that the calculation on the value intrinsic to a share or asset is the primary goal of the whole Fundamental Analysis. After the investor is aware of the information in reality the investor may decide to take on his own investment even knowing whether it was properly counted and what the likely future price trend seen in the market would be.

This is the reason that specialists in this field have been trying to develop different models that allow investors to track more easily the true value. Some models require a complex set of steps, that can result in errors as well as an wrong results.

It is however possible to change the models back down to two kinds: Dividend Discount Models which are also known as dividend discounting models in addition to those that are Stock Market Multiples, known as models of market multiples. Each model has experienced significant modifications through the years that have resulted in an overall improvement of the whole Fundamental Analysis.

3.2.1 The model of dividend discounting

Dividend Discount Models Dividend Discount Models concentrate on discounting the final cost of a particular financial instrument, and the discounting of any dividends paid within a specific period of time that coincides with the time of ownership of the instrument. This discounting is inevitably dependent on the interest rate which is calculated using other analysis tools, for instance CAPM model. CAPM Model (Capital Asset Pricing Model).

The reasoning behind the model rests on understanding and study of balance sheet information that are made available by businesses, from which one can draw the hypothetical intrinsic value of financial security. The value calculated can be compared to that of the market, in order to determine if it's real and reliable, as well as to figure out if the business is overvalued or undervalued.

3.2.2 Method of Market Multiples

The same results that can be obtained using the dividend discounting method could be obtained using the market multiples method which is among the most commonly used methods utilized for traders to arrive at an accurate business valuation. The method is based on the evaluation of costs of the goods manufactured by companies that are similar to the same industry. The prices that are analyzed are linked to the elements on the balance sheet, including the profits, but also those of EBITDA, EBIT and shareholders equity. In this way, different multiples emerge.

The most crucial and frequently utilized multiple for traders is the ratio of price to the average profit of the industry. In general it is the historical profit that is utilized, however the most accurate indicator can be obtained through comparing the price to the anticipated profits for the year in question. This market multiplier provides crucial details about the number of years needed to pay back only the gains from investment made by the company. A low number in the report means an undervaluation of the business. while high values suggest that the company is valued too high. There isn't a benchmark value that a trader could consider to be an ideal value, however the value of the multiple has to be compared with that of the industry of reference. In actual fact an older sector will have lower ratios between earnings and price, while due to the high expectation of growth, younger sectors have a greater average ratio.

Multiple also refers to the relation between equity and price. You can calculate net assets by calculating the differences between the assets and liabilities and also by adding reserves listed in the statements to the capitalization of the shares. The business valuation method is typically used to determine the actual value of assets of the assets held by insurance, financial or banking institutions. The report assists traders to comprehend the value at which the market will accept a profit in relation to the worth of assets of the company.

If the report shows an outcome lower than If the report gives a lower value, the business is overvalued, and it is a lower value that is reported in markets than the actual one. If you look at the opposite when the report gives an amount less than 0.5 and the valuation of the company is extremely low and the multiple could indicate the possibility of a real crisis.

3.3 - - The real property sector

One of the primary indicators of the the market's health is the real estate industry. This is one of the biggest sources from which traders can get a wealth of information, particularly with regards to long-term investments.

The significance in the property market is mostly due to its immense influence at the macroeconomic as well as at the microeconomic level. Particularly, the first is among the most important indicators of the future development that an economy may hide and the other is an indicator of valuation of portfolios among individuals.

In general the real estate market is viewed as an evaluation unit composed of buildings and land on it. However, the appraisal does not take into account this aspect and instead focuses on the intention of use which is to determines if the property is meant for commercial or residential.

Like almost every other asset, including the real estate market there is the possibility to invest over the long term as well as speculative investments that could turn into profit over the medium and short time. Particularly investors speculate in the real estate market by purchasing a home at an amount lower than the actual value of the property this can happen in the course of an auction for real estate, and then sell the property at the correct price, within the shortest amount of time.

The other thing that connects the real estate industry to finance is availability of credit. In actuality, the acquisition or construction of a house is the primary reason an entity that funds the property gives a loan to a private person in the same way that the purchase or the realization in the realization of properties that are productive is the main reason behind the granting of corporate mortgages, or the agreement of leasing contracts. Due to the close connection to real estate as well as the interest cost that property prices can be susceptible to extreme volatility and has a major impact on the market for stocks. Banks and credit institutions are able to maintain an unreserved reserve that is tied by the quality and quality of credit that they provide. Any decline in the value of the real estate market could result in very negative effects that could result in severe financial crisis, like the one that which occurred within 2009 in the United States in 2009.

So, a fundamental analysis has to constantly observe the entire real estate market to know which events could impact the financial markets, and which have only indirect effects. To make this easier each state has designed an system to continuously monitor the real estate industry. These systems permit you to gather certain data, either quarterly or monthly depending on the country, as well as the different cities, municipalities urban conglomerates, cities, and metropolitan cities. With this information, the analyst is able to more quickly and accurately determine the price trends that are currently in place is in the market and can develop forecasts for potential future changes.

The entity that performs this function for the United States is the S&P Case In the European region, Eurostat is the one that provides the information. In Japan the study that is made accessible to any potential analysts, traders , and investors is performed entirely by the Ministry which is responsible for both the state of the country and infrastructure. The Ministry has separated the study of the market for real estate into two distinct types:

the first is exclusively dedicated to deep studies conducted on the market, and also to the interpretations that relate to the developments of the different patterns, while the other is devoted to the analysis of pure statistics.

In order to open an investment of the real estate , it's possible to use two kinds of execution. The first is direct , and requires a substantial capital reserve, as well as a continuous and ongoing control for the investments. The capital that is allocated may be derived from the owner or by loans and loans given. Another option is the possibility of purchasing the property, but not holding the entire property however, it is only a part of an investment fund. Due to a variety of reasons, the usage of mutual funds is different from the other. Actually, this second method to open an investment takes considerably less time and less commitment. Additionally, the expenses associated with the management as well as for the different commissions that are associated with the project are divided in accordance with the quota that is set. Another benefit is the possibility of splitting the risk. In reality an investment fund like this one is one that divides capital across a huge amount of assets, giving the chance of investing in markets that are far away.

Alongside the direct data that the real estate market provides, it also provides some indirect information that needs to be taken in and analyzed by the analyst who is fundamental. In reality the real estate indexes could be used as benchmarks and provide an fascinating basis for analysis to predict what the future direction of the different financial instruments that are analyzed.

3.4 Analytical Fundamentals in Forex

In Forex fundamental analysts are required to have the aim of determining what the future trends in the price of financial instruments on the market could be. To accomplish this objective it is essential to be aware of various factors that constantly impact the market and are able to influence the the financial market trends.

One of the primary elements that every essential analyst has to study is interest rates. The amount of this component is determined by central banks in every country, and they act in accordance with the logic used by the different governments. It is therefore inevitable that the decisions made in this field will can have an impact on the Forex market, particularly when it is a country with a significant influence at the global scale.

Inflation is a different aspect which should not be ignored. This is the measure of worth and power of purchasing of money and is consequently, an essential element of any financial market. In this instance governments, by various strategies, can influence in the amount of inflation being aware that a higher rate will result in a reduction in consumption, whereas the rate that is too low can lead to recession.

Naturally, any important analyst that is involved on the Forex market must be able to relate to the country's GDP. It is essential to analyze this aspect in order to know what the degree of volatility on the market. Furthermore, GDP is regarded as to be one of the key indicators of the performance of economics of a country. Analysts who study fundamentals can also utilize the preliminary GDP ratios without waiting for an official report, to determine if there is a possibility of a trend change, and earn substantial gains.

However, Forex also has roots within the social system, and for that reason the rate of unemployment is among the most significant indicators of price changes. Alongside being an crucial indicator of the general health of a nation the rate of unemployment shows the amount of wealth that is held by individuals, which can impact GDP and consumption of the country.

A nation that has excellent economic and social wellbeing has an impressive balance in trade which is the result of the gap between the exports and imports that occur over a certain time. In addition, if the imports are greater than exports and the value of the currency will increase and in the reverse situation, the currency is weaker.

The stability of the government is among the major factors that affect the fluctuation within Forex. Naturally, the faith placed by traders who are not able to trust the government in their the domestic financial stock market results in prices fluctuating.

In addition to these variables and scenarios every trader has to concentrate their analyses of financials on 3 additional factors. They either directly or indirectly affect the market and demand an in-depth and thorough analysis.

3.4.1 the Monetary Policy of Central Banks

Analyzing the Monetary Policy moves implemented by central banks at different levels is crucial to grasp the actual possibilities within a state , a trend toward economic growth may be created. It is important to understand that the Monetary Policy does not only perform its duties in the area of interest rates and inflation but also addresses the interaction to other countries, technological investments, and social welfare. It is, therefore, an extremely broad field that covers almost all aspects of the economy. But, each decision is made and carried out by the central banks, who are governed by the political agenda of the government and based on rules of central banks around the world.

3.4.2 The economy

Traders also need to be able to base their analysis on factors that affect the performance of an economy group of nations or a nation. This kind of analysis should be based on all of the aspects of politics and society that define a region as well as the consumption level of the nation as well as the various productive sectors. Thus economics is among the main pillars which support the complete Fundamental Analysis of Forex and for the purpose of analyzing it thoroughly, traders will need to dedicate considerable time and effort to this stage of analysis, or use the data already in place however, they may incorrect or inaccurate.

3.4.3 The current trend in oil and gold commodities

The oil and gold are two items that have the most impact on the financial industry and the Forex market. These two components are often overlooked, ignored and are not considered in analysis, however they are vital in determining the future trends of the market could be.

Gold is often considered to be the best refuge in the world. That means that investors should, in the event of markets experience negative times, are advised to put money into gold. This is why that even though most financial instruments exhibit negative trends however, gold is the only thing that can show an upward trend. However, gold displays negative trends when the market is in a state of excitement.

Oil is also among the most influential commodities on the world's markets and especially the Forex. There are two types of oil. The suggestion is to concentrate at West Texas Intermediate, also called WTI that is more influential over Brent. Brent.

In reality, nearly all global economies depend on oil, whether they import it, or because they export it which means this significance will eventually spill onto the financial market. A decrease in the price of oil will therefore bring advantages for countries that import oil and in the case of exporting countries, a disadvantage in reverse.

Chapter 15: The Definition, Process And The

Purpose Of Technical Analysis

The field of technical analysis is where future trends of currency pairs, securities and crypto currencies are analyzed from patterns in the past. In simple terms, it involves using the past to determine the future. The past, then is examined through the variety of patterns and indicators in charts. In terms of technical analysis spans a long time and the fundamental principles were first implemented by an Dutch trader called Joseph de la Vega in the 17th century. The same time frame trading on Japan's rice markets came up with similar concepts. Early writing on the field of behavioral economics, trends and the development that of the chart using candlesticks could be also be attributed to Japan and the rice futures market. Techniques of analysis could be seen in texts dating in time to Imperial China and ancient Babylon. More recently the modern technique of technical analysis is mostly due in large part, to Charles Dow. Many of his ideas as well as others developed into a mature and common type of analysis by the late 20th century.

The Key Three

If you've got an notion about what technical analysis actually is and what it is, you must equip with a technological (no no pun meant) analysis with an ideology-driven basis that is the logic analysts use to trade. This is done by using "the crucial three." The three keys are a collection of popular phrases (as academics would call them, "premises") that define the logic behind technical analysis. The majority of everything that is related to analysis of technical aspects including indicators, studying charts and even the complete foundation of purchasing and selling investments which is based on the past, is based on these assertions. We will start by addressing the first.

1. History Repeats Itself

Although the notion that history is prone to repeat itself is self-explanatory however, it's an original concept. Think about the question: why does history have to repeat itself (history solely about investments)? There aren't any laws that demand the price of investments to behave in a particular manner. There is no inherent intelligence that can guide historical movements regarding the future or present movement. But, the entire base is the fact the fact that historical events repeat themselves which means that it is possible to predict the course of history. If the future is predicted, then the possibility of making money is there. This is, assuming that the above tendency to repetition are result of external influences, specifically, those who invest themselves.

2. The Market Reduces Everything

The notion that the market is a discount on everything, usually referred to as "market action is a discount on everything," is part of the Efficient market Hypothesis (EMH). The EMH claims the fact that price (within our own context, for instance that is, the price of cryptocurrency) are a reflection of all the information available. Different versions of this theory exist, that are believed to be to be strong, weak, or all in between. In particular, because it is extremely unstable and influenced by trends more than other markets for security and is therefore less effective because prices and price rises may not accurately reflect the true value. For instance If Elon Musk tweets about a small-cap crypto , and the price is trending 500% higher it could be said that the price hike isn't a true reflection of an efficient market since the real worth of the project didn't change. But, the notion that the market may not be completely efficient is a good idea because it opens opportunities for undervalued projects. The analysis of technical aspects, for instance seeks to determine discounted prices by using techniques. But, when we return to the initial statement that the market discountes everything suggests that the vast majority of future actions already reflect in the price currently. For instance, if the company X is scheduled to launch an app within thirty days time, then the price already shows this fact even though it's not happening yet. In the event that this happens at a greater scale it's logical to conclude that the only analysis that is important is the study of price movements as random factors like announcements can't be predicted in the future. Therefore, technical analysts are concerned more about what's most likely to occur in the context of historical events rather than what might occur based on data already included in securities (such as trading on the basis of the news, trends, earnings and so on.). This type of trading can be self-fulfilling since it is a fact that, in a certain manner traders design the events they believe will occur by trading as though those things happen.

3. Prices Change in Trends

The concept of trends is a vital concept for technical analysts. An analyst who is a technical one must believe that prices and prices move in a trend, because otherwise, the whole purpose of charting price changes is invalidated. Therefore, it is essential to believe that prices are moving in the direction of trends and tend to stay in trend in the opposite direction than reverse.

As a trader in technical markets one should believe that the past repeats itself, the market is a discounter of every thing, while prices change in a direction. These three assertions form the foundational ideology upon the basis of all analysis in technical fields. built.

Different types of indicators

Chart Patterns

A lot of indicators have patterns in charts. Charts, on the other hand are simply the movement of prices between up and down, which is price action. Price action that is predictable is a pattern. patterns can be used as an accurate indicator.

www.ingramcontent.com/pod-product-compliance
Lightning Source LLC
LaVergne TN
LVHW012201220225
804335LV00008B/526